MEDIÆVAL HYMNS

AND

Sequences.

TRANSLATED BY

THE REV. J. M. NEALE, D.D.,
WARDEN OF SACKVILLE COLLEGE.

Second Edition,
WITH VERY NUMEROUS ADDITIONS AND CORRECTIONS.

"loquendi
Cura de Sanctis vitiosa non est.
Nec rudis unquam."
PRUDENTIUS.

LONDON:
JOSEPH MASTERS, ALDERSGATE STREET,
AND NEW BOND STREET.
MDCCCLXIII.

DEDICATED

TO THE

REVEREND THOMAS HELMORE, M.A.,

PRIEST IN ORDINARY TO THE QUEEN,
PRECENTOR OF S. MARK'S COLLEGE, ETC., ETC.,

AS A MARK OF GRATITUDE

FOR HIS LABOURS IN THE REFORMATION OF

Ecclesiastical Music.

PREFACE.

THE ten years which have elapsed since the first edition of the present little work have done very much for the science of Hymnology. They have witnessed the publication, in Germany, of Mone's three volumes, of Daniel's fourth and fifth, and of Cunz's Geschichte des Deutschen Kirchenliedes: in France, of Gautier's Adam of S. Victor: in England, of my own *Sequentiæ Medii Ævi*, and the yet unfinished series of *Sequentiæ Ineditæ* in the "Ecclesiologist."

During the same period at least sixty different hymnals have issued from the press, the most memorable being the Hymnal Noted, the Sarum Hymnal, Hymns Ancient and Modern, Mr. Chope's Collection, and Sir Roundell Palmer's Book of Praise. Though not a Hymnal, it would be unjust not to mention Mr. J. D. Chambers' translation of

the Sarum Breviary, with the new translation
of its Hymns.

It would be, I think, merely unthankful to
Him from Whom all good things come, did I
not express my gratitude for the great favour
He has given so many of my translations, (both
in this and other works) in the English Church:
and more especially, "Jerusalem the Golden,"
"To thee, O dear dear country," "The strain
upraise," "CHRIST is made the sure foundation," and "The Royal Banners." That they
have been a good deal altered in their various
transcriptions was only to be expected; and I
hope that the remarks which I have here and
there made in the following pages on some of
these alterations, will not be taken, as I am
sure they were not meant, unkindly. In some
instances I thankfully acknowledge them to be
improvements: in some I think that had the
reproducers studied the Commentaries of Clich-
toveus and Nebrissensis, they would have left the
original as it was: I will give an example or
two. In the glorious *Ad Cœnam Agni providi*
the last word of the first line is undoubtedly
the nominative case plural:

> The LAMB's high banquet *we await*,

as it is in the Hymnal Noted. But in most

reproductions that line is altered, I suppose from the editors' either not seeing or not believing that the adjective applies to ourselves, not to the LAMB.

Again, in the same Hymn :—

Cruore ejus roseo

is translated by

And tasting of His roseate Blood.

The epithet is everywhere altered to *Crimson*: because the editors did not see its force. The poet would tell us that, though one drop of our LORD'S Blood was sufficient to redeem the world,

(Cujus una stilla salvum facere
Totum mundum quit ab omni scelere,

as S. Thomas says,) yet out of the greatness of His love to us He would shed all. As every one knows, the last drainings of life-blood are not crimson, but of a far paler hue: strictly speaking, *roseate*. Change the word, and you eliminate the whole idea.

Some of the happiest and most instructive hours of my life were spent in the Sub-Committee of the Ecclesiological Society, appointed for the purpose of bringing out the Second Part of the Hymnal Noted. It was my business to lay before it the translations I had prepared, and theirs to correct. The study which this required drew out the beauties of the original in a way which nothing else could have done, and the friendly collision of various minds elicited ideas which a single translator would, in all probability, have missed.   I have been amused to find, in some reproductions of these hymns, a line given as I had at first written it, to the exclusion of our deliberate correction. If any one cares to see how much the hymns were improved by the process, he may compare the two of Venantius Fortunatus, as they stand in the first and in the present edition of this book.

There is only one thing with respect to the use of any of my hymns that has grieved me ; the rejection of the noble melody of the Alleluiatic Sequence, and that for a third-rate chant. What would be said of chanting the *Dies Iræ*? And yet I really believe that it would suffer less than does the *Cantemus cuncti* by such a substitution. Further, be it noticed, every sentence, I had almost said every word, of the version was carefully fitted to the music : the length of the lines corresponds to the length of each *troparion* in

the original :—and these are now stretched
on the Procrustean bed of the same meaning-
less melody. That the original music cannot be
learnt in an hour or two is most certain : but
seeing that I have heard it thoroughly well
sung, and most heartily enjoyed, by a school
choir, varying in ages from fourteen to five, is
it not unworthy of the great choral meetings,
as at Ely, Salisbury, Sherborne, and elsewhere,
including the words in their programmes, so
utterly to spoil them in their performance?
Let it be remembered that I have some little
right to speak on the subject, having been the
first to introduce the Sequence to English
readers, and there being, even now, no other
translation but my own. I will only add, that
I could, and gladly would, procure the oppor-
tunity of hearing it sung by the Choir of a
London church for any Choir master who may
be desirous of introducing it into his own.

I felt that the best return I could make for
the great kindness with which hymns from
this little volume and others of mine have been
received was to spare no pains in improving
them as far as I possibly could. And above
all have I endeavoured to do this in Adam of
S. Victor, to my mind the greatest Latin poet,

not only of mediæval, but of all, ages. It is a
magnificent thing to pass along the far-stretch-
ing vista of Hymns,—from the sublime self-
containedness of S. Ambrose to the more
fervid inspiration of S. Gregory, the exquisite
typology of Venantius Fortunatus, the lovely
painting of S. Peter Damiani, the crystal-like
simplicity of S. Notker, the scriptural calm
of Godescalcus, the subjective loveliness of
S. Bernard, till all culminate in the full blaze
of glory which surrounds Adam of S. Victor,
the greatest of all. And though Thomas of
Celano in one unapproachable Sequence dis-
tanced him, and the author, whoever he were,
of the *Verbum Dei Deo natum* once equalled
him, what are we to think of the genius that
could pour forth one hundred Sequences, of
which fifty at least are unequalled save by the
Dies Iræ?

When the first edition of my book was
published, Gautier's collection of the works of
Adam had not appeared :—and several of them
were yet MS. Two out of these, the *Stola
Regni laureatus*, and the *Verbi vere substantivi*,
will be found here. Probably no poet is so
hard to translate, from the subtleness of his
allusions, the richness of his rhyme, the close

way in which he packs his meaning. And
I am therefore bound to express my deep
gratitude to the first Victorine scholar in Eng-
land, and probably in Europe, the Dean of
Westminster, for his criticisms and alterations.
At p. 126 are these lines :

> Whom Luke's pen, true ox-horn, sheweth
> On the Cross whence healing floweth:

Dr. Trench pointed out to me that in the
original

> Quem exaltat super cruce
> Cornu bovis, penna Lucæ,

I had omitted the force of the *exaltat* as taken
in connection with the *cornu*, and proposed—
unfortunately too late for me to insert it in the
text,—what I should wish to be read there :

> Whom Luke's pen, true ox-horn, lifted
> On the Cross with healing gifted.

Indeed, Adam is worth any pains and any
study :—and if any reader thinks it worth while
to compare the translations from him in the
first and second editions of my book, he will see,
I think, that they have not been spared.

One more observation remains to be made.
I have kept strictly to the rule of adopting the
exact measure and rhyme of the original,—at
whatever inconvenience and cramping. The

only exception is that, in Trochaics of this character :

In Patre potentia cuncta denotatur
Filio prudentia omnis declaratur :
Gratia Paraclito universa datur,
Qui cum Patre Natoque congiorificatur,

where they rhyme, as here, in quatrains, I have usually rhymed them in couplets.

Dean Trench has, in his Calderon, some most excellent remarks on this subject, to which I would refer the reader.

And to what is there said, must be added the terrible loss thereby sustained through the loss of the original melodies. Many of the modern books, for instance, oblige him that employs them, for example, in the beautiful *Jesu dulcis memoria*, to forego the exquisite Sarum Christmas melody to which it was sung as a hymn in the old English Church :—and the still more exquisite sequence melody to which it belonged when a prose :—a melody which I have heard every Sunday after evening service for more than six years, and love more dearly every time I do hear it. He cannot sing the *Ad Cœnam Agni providi* to its own noble tune : nor, as I have said, the Alleluiatic Sequence : and so of several others. It

is from this defect that popular, and in many
respects deservedly popular, as Hymns Ancient
and Modern are now, I cannot but believe
that, as the science of Hymnology deepens
it will either have to reform itself in this par-
ticular, or to make way to a rival which shall
observe this all-important rule.

I can only repeat, in conclusion, how sorry I
should be if anything either in the above preface, or in the notes, gives pain, and that no
one can be more thankful than I should be
for any criticism of which I may avail myself in (should it be called for) a future
edition.

SACKVILLE COLLEGE,
 S. Stephen, 1862.

PAGE

*AUDI NOS, REX CHRISTE. Eleventh Century . 50

*GRAVI ME TERRORE PULSAS, VITÆ DIES ULTIMA.
S. *Peter Damiani.* Died 1072 . . . 52

*CRUX MUNDI BENEDICTIO. *S. Peter Damiani.*
Died 1072 55

*CIVES CŒLESTIS PATRIÆ. *Marbodus of Rennes.*
Died 1125 57

*HORA NOVISSIMA. *Bernard of Cluny.* Twelfth
Century 68

*PATRIS SAPIENTIA, BONITAS DIVINA. Twelfth
Century 93

*CŒNAM CUM DISCIPULIS. Twelfth Century . 99

*JUCUNDARE, PLEBS FIDELIS. *Adam of S. Victor.*
Died 1192 106

*ECCE DIES CELEBRIS. *Adam of S. Victor* . . 114

*ZYMA VETUS EXPURGETUR. *Adam of S. Victor* 118

¶VERBI VERE SUBSTANTIVI. *Adam of S Victor* . 125

†SUPERNÆ MATRIS GAUDIA. *Adam of S. Victor* 128

†INTERNI FESTI GAUDIA. *Adam of S. Victor* . 131

†HERI MUNDUS EXULTAVIT. *Adam of S. Victor* 134

¶MISSUS GABRIEL DE CŒLIS. *Adam of S. Victor* 137

*LAUDES CRUCIS ATTOLLAMUS. *Adam of S. Victor* 139

*QUAM DILECTA TABERNACULA. *Adam of S. Victor* 146

¶STOLA REGNI LAUREATUS. *Adam of S. Victor*. 153

*IN HOC ANNI CIRCULO. ⎫ 158

O FILII ET FILIÆ. ⎪ 163

*SURREXIT CHRISTUS HODIE. ⎬ Apparently 166
                          of the
*FINITA JAM SUNT PRŒLIA. ⎪ Twelfth 168
                          Century.
*JAM PULSA CEDUNT NUBILA. ⎪ 170

*VENI, VENI, EMMANUEL. ⎪ 171

*CŒLOS ASCENDIT HODIE. ⎭ 173

*ECCE TEMPUS EST VERNALE. Thirteenth Century 174

PAGE

ADORO TE DEVOTE, LATENS DEITAS. *S. Thomas Aquinas.* Died 1274 176
PANGE LINGUA GLORIOSI. *S. Thomas Aquinas.* 178
ALLELUIA, DULCE CARMEN. Thirteenth Century 182
*DIES EST LÆTITIÆ 185
*NOVI PARTUS GAUDIUM 187
†O QUAM GLORIFICUM 190
¶MULTI SUNT PRESBYTERI. Fourteenth Century 194
*OMNIS FIDELIS GAUDEAT 200
*GLORIOSI SALVATORIS. Fifteenth Century . 202
†REDEUNDO PER GYRUM 204
*O BEATA BEATORUM 208
†ÆSTIMAVIT HORTOLANUM 210
*TANDEM FLUCTUS, TANDEM LUCTUS . . 212
*ATTOLLE PAULLUM LUMINA. ⎫ Fifteenth ⎧ 214
*EXITE, SION FILIÆ.   ⎪ or ⎪ 217
*HUC AD JUGUM CALVARIÆ. ⎬ Sixteenth ⎨ 220
*TRIUMPHE! PLAUDANT MARIA. ⎭ Century. ⎩ 223

N.B. An asterisk means that the piece here trans-lated had never received an English version from a previous writer.

A † that it was not contained in the first edition of the present book.

And ¶ that it has never been printed anywhere till in this second edition.

MEDIÆVAL HYMNS,

Pange lingua gloriosi.

Venantius Fortunatus, whose life extended from
530 to 609, is the connecting link between the poetry
of Sedulius and Prudentius, and that of the middle
ages. The friend of S. Gregory of Tours and S. Radegund, he long wandered over the South of France,
the fashionable poet of his day. The latter half of his
life, however, raised him to a higher post, and to a
holier character. He died bishop of Poitiers. The
following is in the very first class of Latin Hymns:
and is retained, with a few ill-judged retouchings, in
the Roman Breviary.

SING, my tongue, the glorious battle,[1]
　　With completed victory rife:
And above the Cross's trophy.
　　Tell the triumph of the strife:
How the world's Redeemer conquer'd
　　By surrendering of His Life.

B

God his Maker, sorely grieving
  That the first-made Adam fell,
When he ate the fruit of sorrow,
  Whose reward was death and hell,
Noted then this Wood, the ruin
  Of the ancient wood to quell.

For the work of our Salvation
  Needs would have his order so,
And the multiform deceiver's
  Art by art would overthrow,
And from thence would bring the med'cine
  Whence the insult of the foe.

Wherefore, when the sacred fulness
  Of th' appointed time was come,
This world's Maker left His Father,
  Sent the Heavenly Mansion from,
And proceeded, God Incarnate,
  Of the Virgin's Holy Womb.

Weeps the Infant in the manger
  That in Bethlehem's stable stands;
And His Limbs the Virgin Mother
  Doth compose in swaddling bands,
Meetly thus in linen folding
  Of her God the feet and hands.

Thirty years among us dwelling,
  His appointed time fulfill'd,
Born for this, He meets his Passion,
  For that this He freely will'd:
On the Cross the LAMB is lifted,
  Where His life-blood shall be spilled.

He endured the nails, the spitting,
  Vinegar, and spear, and reed;
From that Holy Body broken
  Blood and water forth proceed:
Earth, and stars, and sky, and ocean,
  By that flood from stain are freed.

Faithful Cross! above all other,
  One and only noble tree!
None in foliage, none in blossom,
  None in fruit thy peers may be:
Sweetest Wood, and sweetest Iron!
  Sweetest Weight is hung on thee.

Bend thy boughs, O Tree of Glory!
  Thy relaxing sinews bend;
For awhile the ancient rigour,
  That thy birth bestowed, suspend;
And the King of Heavenly Beauty
  On thy bosom gently tend!

Thou alone wast counted worthy
    This world's ransom to uphold ;
For a shipwrecked race preparing
    Harbour, like the Ark of old ;
With the sacred Blood anointed
    From the smitten LAMB that roll'd.[2]

To the TRINITY be glory
    Everlasting, as is meet :
Equal to the FATHER, equal
    To the SON, and PARACLETE :
Trinal Unity, Whose praises
    All created things repeat.   Amen.

----

[1] The recension of Urban VIII. here entirely spoils
the original,

            Pange lingua gloriosi
            Prælium certaminis,

by substituting the word *Lauream*. It is not to the
glory of the termination of our LORD's conflict with
the Devil that the poet would have us look : but to
the glory of the struggle itself : as indeed he tells us
at the conclusion of the verse.

* A verse is added by some which, though not original, seems ancient :

> When, O Judge of this world, coming
> In Thy glory all divine,
> Thou shalt bid Thy Cross's Trophy
> Bright above the stars to shine,
> Be the Light and the Salvation
> Of the people that are Thine !

[The translation as it stood in the first edition was adopted, with a few improvements, in the *Hymnal Noted*. Those improvements are retained here, as they will be in the like cases through the present volume.]

Vexilla Regis prodeunt.

This world-famous hymn, one of the grandest in
the treasury of the Latin Church, was composed by
Fortunatus, on occasion of the reception of certain
relics by S. Gregory of Tours and S. Radegund, pre-
viously to the consecration of a church at Poitiers.
It is therefore strictly and primarily a processional
hymn, though very naturally afterwards adapted to
Passiontide.

THE Royal Banners forward go ;
The Cross shines forth in mystic glow ;
Where He in flesh, our flesh Who made,
Our sentence bore, our ransom paid.

Where deep for us the spear was dy'd,
Life's torrent rushing from His side,
To wash us in that precious flood
Where mingled Water flow'd, and Blood.

Fulfill'd is all that David told
In true Prophetic song of old ;
Amidst the nations GOD, saith he,
Hath reign'd and triumph'd from the Tree.[1]

O Tree of Beauty! Tree of Light!
O Tree with royal purple dight!
Elect on whose triumphal breast
Those holy limbs should find their rest!

On whose dear arms, so widely flung,
The weight of this world's ransom hung:
The price of human kind to pay,
And spoil the Spoiler of his prey.

[O Cross, our one reliance, hail!
This holy Passiontide, avail
To give fresh merit to the Saint,
And pardon to the penitent.

To Thee, Eternal Three in one,
Let homage meet by all be done;
Whom by the Cross Thou dost restore,
Preserve and govern evermore.][a]

———————

[1] In the Italic Version the tenth verse of the 96th Psalm is—"Tell it out among the heathen that the LORD reigneth from the Tree." S. Justin Martyr accuses the Jews of corrupting the text; and Tertullian, in at least three places, quotes the older reading.

[2] These verses were added when the Hymn was appropriated to Passiontide. The ending of Fortunatus is this:

> With fragrance dropping from each bough
> Sweeter than sweetest nectar thou:
> Decked with the fruit of peace and praise,
> And glorious with Triumphal lays :—
>
> Hail, Altar! Hail, O Victim! Thee
> Decks now Thy Passion's Victory;
> Where Life for sinners death endured,
> And life by death for man procured.

The two last lines are substituted in the modern Roman Breviary for the concluding half of the first verse. The poet had possibly the distich of Sedulius in his eye.

> Vita beata necem miseris avertere venit:
> Pertulit a miseris Vita beata necem.

[This translation was also adopted in the Hymnal Noted, from whence it was copied into *Hymns Ancient and Modern*, with some alterations which, I think, are not improvements: *e.g.* in ver. 3, we have the colloquialism of—" Fulfilled is now *what* David told."]

Apparebit repentina magna Dies Domini.

This rugged, but grand Judgment Hymn,[1] is at least as early as the 7th century, because quoted by V. Bede. It manifestly contains the germ of the *Dies Iræ*, to which, however inferior in lyric fervour and effect, it scarcely yields in devotion and simple realisation of its subject. In the original it is acrostic.

THAT great Day of wrath and terror,
That last Day of woe and doom,
Like a thief that comes at midnight,
On the sons of men shall come;
When the pride and pomp of ages
All shall utterly have pass'd,
And they stand in anguish, owning
That the end is here at last;
And the trumpet's pealing clangour,
Through the earth's four quarters spread,
Waxing loud and ever louder,
Shall convoke the quick and dead:
And the King of heavenly glory
Shall assume His throne on high,

And the cohorts of His angels
Shall be near Him in the sky :
And the sun shall turn to sackcloth,
And the moon be red as blood,
And the stars shall fall from heaven,
Whelm'd beneath destruction's flood.
Flame and fire, and desolation
At the Judge's feet shall go :
Earth and sea, and all abysses
Shall His mighty sentence know.
Then the elect upon the right hand
Of the LORD shall stand around ;
But, like goats, the evil doers
Shall upon the left be found :
" Come, ye Blessed, take the kingdom,"
Shall be there the King's award,
" Which for you, before the world was,
Of My FATHER was prepared :
I was naked, and ye clothed Me ;
Poor, and ye relieved Me ; hence
Take the riches of My glory
For your endless recompense."
.Then the righteous shall make question,—
" When have we beheld Thee poor,
LORD of glory ?   When relieved Thee
Lying needy at our door ?"
Whom the Blessed King shall answer,—
" When ye showed your charity,

Giving bread and home, and raiment,
What ye did was done to Me."
In like manner to the left hand
That most righteous Judge shall say,
"Go, ye cursed, to Gehenna,
And the fire that is for aye:
For in prison ye came not nigh Me,—
Poor, ye pitied not My lot;
Naked, ye have never clothed Me;
Sick, ye visited Me not."—
They shall say: "O CHRIST, when saw we
That Thou calledst for our aid,
And in prison, or sick, or hungry,
To relieve have we delayed?"
Whom again the Judge shall answer:
"Since ye never cast your eyes
On the sick, and poor, and needy,
It was Me ye did despise."

   Backward, backward, at the sentence,
To Gehenna they shall fly,
Where the flame is never-ending,
Where the worm can never die;
Where are Satan and his angels
In profoundest dungeon bound;
Where are chains and lamentation,
Where are quenchless flames around.

   But the righteous, upward soaring,
To the heavenly Land shall go,

Midst the cohorts of the angels,
Where is joy for evermo :
To Jerusalem, exulting,
They with shouts shall enter in ;
That true "sight of peace" and glory
That sets free from grief and sin.
CHRIST shall they behold for ever,
Seated at the FATHER's hand,
As in Beatific Vision
His elect before Him stand.

    Wherefore, man, while yet thou mayest,
From the dragon's malice fly ;
Give thy bread to feed the hungry,
If thou seek'st to win the sky ;
Let thy loins be straitly girded,
Life be pure, and heart be right ;
At the coming of the Bridegroom,
That thy lamp may glitter bright.

----

[1] There is another hymn, also quoted by V. Bede,
of the same rhythm and style as this ; probably of the
same date, and perhaps by the same author. I should
have added it here, but for its great length. It
begins "Hymnum dicat turba fratrum, hymnum
cantus personet."

Sancti, venite, Corpus Christi sumite.

Rugged and unpoetical as this hymn is, it has a certain pious simplicity about it which renders it well worthy of preservation. It is an early example of a metrical composition, sung during the communion of the people. The *Communio* of the Latin, like the *Koinonicon* of the Eastern, Church, never now appears but as prose.—The present hymn seems not later than the seventh century.

DRAW nigh, and take the Body of the LORD,
And drink the Holy Blood for you outpoured.

Saved by that Body, hallowed by that Blood,
Whereby refreshed, we render thanks to GOD.

Salvation's Giver, CHRIST the Only SON,
By that His Cross and Blood the victory won.

Offered was He for greatest and for least :
Himself the Victim, and Himself the Priest.

Victims were offered by the Law of old,
That, in a type, celestial mysteries told.

He, Ransomer from death, and Light from shade,
Giveth His holy grace His Saints to aid.

Approach ye then with faithful hearts sincere,
And take the safeguard of salvation here.

He That in this world rules His Saints, and
 shields,
To all believers Life Eternal yields:

With Heavenly Bread makes them that hunger
 whole;
Gives Living Waters to the thirsty soul.

Alpha and Omega, to Whom shall bow
All nations at the Doom, is with us now.

Hymnum canentes Martyrum.

A Hymn for the Holy Innocents, the composition of Venerable Bede. Although it stands in unfavourable contrast with the *Salvete flores Martyrum* of Prudentius, it is somewhat strange that no part of it should have been introduced into any English Breviary. It will be observed that the first and last line of every verse are identical. This somewhat frigid conceit, (*Epanalepsis*, as the grammarians call it,) V. Bede seems to have borrowed from the Elegy of Sedulius, which is composed on a similar plan. Other mediæval writers, however, as Peter Damiani, Eugenius of Toledo, Theodulph of Orleans, have employed it.— I have omitted some of the stanzas.

THE Hymn for conquering Martyrs raise :
The Victor Innocents we praise :
Whom in their woe earth cast away,
But Heaven with joy received to-day.
Whose Angels see the FATHER'S Face
World without end, and hymn His Grace :
And while they chant unceasing lays,
The Hymn for conquering Martyrs raise.

By that accursed monarch slain,
Their loving Maker bade them reign :

With Him they dwell, no more distressed,
In the fair Land of light and rest :
He gives them mansions, one and all,
In that His Heavenly FATHER's Hall :
—Thus have they changed their loss for gain,
By that accursed Monarch slain.

A voice from Ramah was there sent,
A voice of weeping and lament :
When Rachel mourned the children's care
Whom for the tyrant's sword she bare.
Triumphal is their glory now
Whom earthly torments could not bow :
What time, both far and near that went,
A voice from Ramah was there sent.

Fear not, O little flock and blest,
The lion that your life oppressed !
To heavenly pastures ever new
The heavenly Shepherd leadeth you ;
Who, dwelling now on Sion's hill
The LAMB's dear footsteps follow still :
By tyrant there no more distressed,
Fear not, O little flock and blest !

And every tear is wiped away
By your dear FATHER's hands for aye ;

Death hath no power to hurt you more,
Whose own is Life's eternal store.—
Who sow their seed, and, sowing, weep,[1]
In everlasting joy shall reap :
What time they shine in heavenly day,
And every tear is wiped away.

O City blest o'er all the earth,
Who gloriest in the SAVIOUR'S birth!
Whose are His earliest Martyrs dear,
By kindred and by triumph here.
None from henceforth may call thee small;—
Of rival towns thou passest all ;
In whom our Monarch had His Birth,—
O City blest o'er all the earth!

---

[1] V. Bede is very fond of a practice not usual
in the Hymns we are considering :—the introducing
the words of Scripture as a part of his own composition :—and the additions he makes to them are
sometimes very beautiful. Here, for example: "Qui
seminant in lacrymis, *Longo* metent in gaudio."
Again, in a fine hymn on the Ascension :

> Mirata adhuc cœlestium
> Rogavit aula Civium :
> Quis (inquit) est Rex gloriæ,
> Rex iste tam laudabilis ?

C

Urbs beata Jerusalem.

This grand Hymn of the eighth century, was modernised in the reform of Pope Urban VIII., into the *Cœlestis Urbs Jerusalem:* and lost half of its beauty in the process.

BLESSED City, Heavenly Salem,
  Vision dear of Peace and Love,
Who, of living stones upbuilded,
  Art the joy of Heav'n above,
And, with angel cohorts circled,
  As a Bride to earth dost move!

From celestial realms descending,
  Ready for the nuptial bed,
To His presence, deck'd with jewels,
  By her LORD shall she be led:
All her streets, and all her bulwarks,
  Of pure gold are fashioned.

Bright with pearls her portal glitters;
  It is open evermore;
And, by virtue of His merits,
  Thither faithful souls may soar,

Who for CHRIST's dear Name, in this world
 Pain and tribulation bore.

Many a blow and biting sculpture
 Polish'd well those stones elect,
In their places now compacted
 By the Heavenly Architect,
Who therewith hath will'd for ever
 That His Palace should be deck'd.

CHRIST is made the sure Foundation,
 And the precious Corner-stone,
Who, the two-fold walls surmounting,
 Binds them closely into one :
Holy Sion's help for ever,
 And her confidence alone.

All that dedicated City,
 Dearly lov'd by GOD on high,
In exultant jubilation
 Pours perpetual melody ;
GOD the One, and GOD the Trinal,
 Singing everlastingly.

To this Temple,[1] where we call Thee,
 Come, O LORD of Hosts, to-day !
With Thy wonted loving-kindness
 Hear Thy people as they pray ;
   c 2

And Thy fullest benediction
  Shed within its walls for aye.

Here vouchsafe to all Thy servants
  That they supplicate to gain :
Here to have and hold for ever
  Those good things their pray'rs obtain ;
And hereafter in Thy Glory
  With Thy blessed ones to reign.

Laud and honour to the FATHER ;
  Laud and honour to the SON ;
Laud and honour to the SPIRIT ;
  Ever Three, and ever ONE :
Consubstantial, Co-eternal,
  While unending ages run.   Amen.[2]

---

[1] Daniel imagines these stanzas to be a later addition, when the hymn, originally general, was adapted to the dedication of a church. Dean Trench, on the contrary, will have the whole poem to be of one date : and alleges, very truly, that this mixture of the earthly and heavenly temple is usual in hymns and sequences on a similar subject. Nevertheless, I think that Daniel is right : 1. Because there is a clear difference in the style and language of the two last and seven first

stanzas. 2. Because the transition from one part to
the other is so unusually abrupt. 3. Because, at the
end of the sixth stanza, there is a quasi-doxology as
if to point out that the hymn originally concluded
there.

² There is, in the Paris Breviary, a *rifacimento* of
this Hymn; very inferior, it is true, to the original,
but much superior to the Roman reform. The first
verse may serve as an example.

Original :

Urbs beata, Jerusálem,
  Dicta pacis visio,
Quæ construitur in cœlo
  Vivis ex lapidibus,
Et angelis coronata
  Ut sponsata comite.

Roman :

Cœlestis urbs Jerusalem
Beata pacis visio,
Quæ celsa de viventibus
Saxis ad astra tolleris ;
Sponsæque ritu cingeris
Mille Angelorum millibus.

Paris :

Urbs beata, vera pacis
  Visio, Jerusalem ;
Quanta surgit ! celsa saxis
  Conditur viventibus :
Quæ polivit, hæc coaptat
  Sedibus suis Deus.

This Hymn, divided as in the Breviary, after the fourth verse, was inserted, with some corrections, in the *Hymnal Noted*. Thence, with a good many alterations, it was copied in the *Sarum Hymnal*: one of these changes seems true and happy : v. 27.

> Who, the two walls underlying,
> Bound in each, binds both in one.

In *Hymns Ancient and Modern* it is very slightly altered : and some of the changes can hardly be thought improvements, e. g., "Thither faithful souls *do* soar." It is curious to observe how both one and the other soften the second line of the second verse : the *Sarum* has :

> Grace and glory round her shed,

Hymns Ancient and Modern, (much better,)

> Bridal glory round her shed.

The second part of the translation, "CHRIST is made the sure Foundation," has been adopted as a dedication hymn with so much general favour, that it would be unthankful not to mention the fact.

Gloria, laus, et honor.

This processional Hymn for Palm Sunday is said to have been composed by S. Theodulph at Metz, or as others will have it, at Angers, while imprisoned on a false accusation: and to have been sung by him from his dungeon window, or by choristers instructed by him, as the Emperor Louis and his Court were on their way to the Cathedral. The good Bishop was immediately liberated. In the original composition there were ten stanzas besides the Chorus. The Roman Missal retains only the first five. Others add, as I have here added, the sixth and the tenth. The remaining three are utterly unworthy of the general beauty of the Hymn.—I have to acknowledge the assistance of a friend in the translation.

GLORY, and honour, and laud be to Thee, King
    CHRIST the Redeemer!
  Children before Whose steps raised their
    Hosannas of praise.
Glory, and honour, &c.

Israel's Monarch art Thou, and the glorious
    Offspring of David,
  Thou that approachest a King blessed in the
    Name of the LORD.
Glory, and honour, &c.

Glory to Thee in the highest the heavenly ar-
    mies are singing:
  Glory to Thee upon earth man and creation
    reply.
Glory, and honour, &c.

Met Thee with Palms in their hands that day
    the folk of the Hebrews:
  We with our prayers and our hymns now
    to Thy presence approach.
Glory, and honour, &c.

They to Thee proffered their praise for to
    herald Thy dolorous Passion;
  We to the King on His Throne utter the
    jubilant hymn.
Glory, and honour, &c.

They were then pleasing to Thee, unto Thee
    our devotion be pleasing;
  Merciful King, kind King, Who in all good-
    ness art pleas'd.
Glory, and honour, &c.

They in their pride of descent were rightly the
    children of Hebrews :
Hebrews[1] are we, whom the LORD's Pass-
    over maketh the same.
Glory, and honour, &c.

Victory won o'er the world be to us for our
    branches of Palm tree :
  So in the Conqueror's joy this to Thee
    still be our song :
Glory, and honour, and laud be to Thee, King
    CHRIST the Redeemer,
  Children before Whose steps raised their
    Hosannas of Praise.

---

[1] This is partly a reference to CHRIST, our True
Passover :—partly to Hebrew, as derived from Heber,
interpreted by passage.

I add another translation, which I made for the
Hymnal Noted.

    Glory, and laud, and honour,
      To Thee, Redeemer King !
    To Whom the lips of children
      Made sweet Hosannas ring !

    Thou art the King of Israel ;
      Thou David's Royal Son ;
    Who in the LORD's Name comest,
      The King and Blessed One.

The Company of Angels
　Are praising Thee on high :
And mortal men, and all things
　Created, make reply.

The people of the Hebrews
　With Palms before Thee went ;
Our praise, and prayer, and anthems
　Before Thee we present.

In hast'ning to Thy Passion,
　They rais'd their hymns of praise :
In reigning 'midst Thy glory,
　Our melody we raise.

Thou didst accept their praises ;
　Accept the prayers we bring,
Who in all good delightest,
　Thou good and gracious King !

This last is adopted in the *Sarum Hymnal*, but with
alterations ; (among which such as in ver. 2, "Our
Blessed King we own," and in ver. 3, "On earth *do*
make reply.") And in *Hymns Ancient and Modern*,
with one change only, and that an improvement ;
(l. 1,) "All glory, laud, and honour."

Another verse was usually sung, till the 17th century ; at the pious quaintness of which we can scarcely
avoid a smile :

Be Thou, O LORD, the Rider,
　And we the little ass ;
That to GOD's Holy City
　Together we may pass.

Tibi, Christe, Splendor Patris.

A Hymn of S. Hrabanus Maurus, Archbishop of
Mayence; born in 777, and deceased in 856. It was
so completely altered in the *Te Splendor et Virtus
Patris* of the modern Roman Breviary, that scarcely
a trace of the original remains. The *Christe qui sedes
Olympo* of Santolius Victorinus in the Parisian Bre-
viary imitates, without equalling, the present hymn.
This is one of the few that have no rhyme.

THEE, O CHRIST, the FATHER'S Splendour,
 Life and virtue of the heart,
In the presence of the Angels
 Sing we now with tuneful art:
Meetly in alternate chorus
 Bearing our responsive part.

Thus we praise with veneration
 All the armies of the sky:
Chiefly him, the warrior Primate
 Of celestial chivalry:
Michael, who in princely virtue
 Cast Abaddon from on high.

By whose watchful care, repelling,
　King of everlasting grace!
Every ghostly adversary,
　All things evil, all things base;
Grant us of Thine only goodness
　In Thy Paradise a place.

Laud and honour to the FATHER;
　Laud and honour to the SON;
Laud and honour to the SPIRIT;
　Ever Three, and ever One:
Consubstantial, Co-eternal,
　While unending ages run.　Amen.

[Adopted in the *Hymnal Noted.*]

𝕾𝖆𝖓𝖈𝖙𝖎 𝕾𝖕𝖎𝖗𝖎𝖙𝖚𝖘 𝖆𝖉𝖘𝖎𝖙 𝖓𝖔𝖇𝖎𝖘 𝖌𝖗𝖆𝖙𝖎𝖆.

We now come to the age of Notkerian Sequences; about which a few words must be said.

It is well known that the origin of sequences themselves is to be looked for in the *Alleluia* of the Gradual, sung between the Epistle and Gospel. During this melody it was necessary that the deacon should have time to ascend from his place at the altar to the rood-loft, that he might thence sing the Gospel. Hence the prolongation of the last syllable in the Alleluia of the Gradual, in thirty, forty, fifty, or even a hundred notes; the *neuma* of which ritualistic writers speak so much. True, there was no sense in this last syllable and its lengthening out, but the mystical interpreters had their explanation: 'the way in which we praise God in our Country is yet unknown.'

And good people were content for some three hundred years with this service; and, as it has been very truly observed, the attempt itself, if one may use the expression, to explain the sound into sense, manifests a little of the rationalism with which the Eastern has always taunted the Western Church. But, towards the beginning of the eleventh century, there was a certain Swiss monk, by name Notker. The defects

of every religious person were well known in the
house where he resided; and a slight lisp in his
speech gave him the surname of *Balbulus*. He had
resided for some years in that marvellous monastery
of S. Gall; the church of which was the pattern of
all monastic edifices, till it was eclipsed by a church,
the description of which now reads like a most
glorious dream—Cluny. While watching the sam-
phire-gatherers on the precipitous cliffs that surrounded S. Gall, Notker had composed the world-
famous hymn, 'In the midst of life we are in death.'
But desirous of obtaining the best education which
Christendom could afford, he afterwards betook himself to the Monastery of Jumièges, and there formed
an acquaintance with many of its monks. With one
of them he had, it seems, a friendly discussion,
whether the interminable *ia* of the Alleluia might
not be altered into a religious sense; a discussion
which, for the time, had no result. But Jumièges,
in common with so many other French monasteries,
was desolated by the barbarian Normans. Where-
upon Notker's friend, bethinking himself of S. Gall,
took refuge in that great house; and the discussion
which years before had commenced, was again carried
on between the two associates. At length Notker
determined to put words to the notes which had
hitherto only interminably prolonged the Alleluia.
He did so : and as a first attempt, produced a sequence
which began with the line—

> ' Laudes Deo concinat orbis universus :'

and which has lately been republished. He brought
this, notes and all, on a parchment rolled round a
cylinder of wood, to Yso, precentor of, what we

should now call the *Cantoris* side. Yso looked kindly
on the composition, but said that he must refer it to
Marcellus, the precentor on the *Decani* side. These
two sang the sequence over together, and observed
that sometimes two notes went to one syllable in a
slur, sometimes three or four syllables went to one
note in a kind of recitative. Yso thereupon was
charged with the message that the verses would not
answer their purpose. Notker, not much discouraged,
revised his composition; and now, instead of (for the
first line) *Laudes Deo concinat orbis universus,* he
substituted, *Laudes Deo concinat orbis ubique totus:*
instead of the second line, *Coluber Adæ deceptor,* he
now wrote, *Coluber Adæ male-suasor:* which as he
himself tells us, when the good-natured Yso had
sung over to himself, he gave thanks to GOD, he
commended the new composition to the brethren of
the monastery, and more especially to Othmar, Yso's
brother by blood. Such then was the origin of sequences, at first called Proses, because written rather
in rhythmical prose than with any attention to metre.

It is impossible in this place to enter into the
extremely elaborate rules of the Notkerians; they
may be seen in my *Epistola de Sequentiis,* prefixed
to the 5th volume of my friend Dr. Daniel's THE-
SAURUS HYMNOLOGICUS.

S. Notker died about 912. The following sequence,
of his composition, was in use all over Europe : even
in those countries, (like Italy and Spain,) which
usually rejected sequences. In the Missal of Palencia
the Priest is ordered to hold a white dove in his
hands, while intoning the first syllables, and then to
let it go.

1. The grace of the HOLY GHOST be present with us;
2. And make our hearts a dwelling place to itself;
3. And expel from them all spiritual wickedness.
4. Merciful SPIRIT, Illuminator of men,
5. Purge the fearful shades of our mind.
6. O holy Lover of thoughts that are ever wise,
7. Of Thy mercy pour forth Thine Anointing into our senses.
8. Thou purifier of all iniquities, O SPIRIT,
9. Purify the eye of our inner man,
10. To the end that the FATHER of all things may be seen by us,
11. He, Whom the eyes of none save the pure in heart can behold.
12. Thou didst inspire the Prophets to chant aforehand their glorious heralding of CHRIST.
13. Thou didst confirm the Apostles, so that they shall bear CHRIST'S glorious trophy through the whole world.
14. When, by His Word, GOD made the system of heaven, earth, seas,
15. Thou didst stretch out Thy Godhead over the waters, and didst cherish them, O SPIRIT!

16. Thou dost give virtue to the waters to quicken souls ;

17. Thou, by Thine Inspiration, grantest to men to be spiritual,

18. Thou didst unite the world, divided both in tongues and rites, O LORD !

19. Thou recallest idolaters to the worship of GOD, best of Masters !

20. Wherefore of Thy mercy hear us who call upon Thee, HOLY GHOST :

21. Without Whom, as the faith teaches, all our prayers are in vain, and unworthy of the ears of GOD.

22. Thou, O SPIRIT, Who by embracing the Saints of all ages, dost teach them by the impulse of Thy Divinity ;

23. Thyself, by bestowing on the Apostles of CHRIST a gift immortal, and unheard of from all ages,

24. Hast made this day glorious.

D

Laus Tibi, Christe.

Next to S. Notker himself, the most famous writer
of the Proses named from him, was Godescalcus—
to be carefully distinguished from his predestinarian
namesake. The following sequence for S. Mary Magdalene is his composition; and has an interesting
notice in the Lives of the Brothers of the Common
Life, by Thomas à Kempis. It occurs in that of Lubert
ten Bosche.

"It fell out also that Master Lubert was seized with
the same plague. And, behold, in the month of July,
three days before the feast of the blessed Mary Magdalene, he fell ill, and took to his bed, and said that
he was not long for this world. We, on the other
hand, laboured with many prayers, and sought reme-
dies from GOD, and from intelligent surgeons, because his life was desirable to all.

"But his prayers were heard beyond ours, and they
were full of desires to be admitted among the heavenly
citizens. One of the brethren said, 'We shall not be
separated so quickly, but we shall hold our conversa-
tions in the room of Master Florentius.' 'No,' said
he, 'not any more here, but in the heavenly places
with the Saints,' for he desired to depart, and to be
with CHRIST. On the feast of S. Mary Magdalene he
asked that the Sequence ' Laus Tibi, Christe,' might
be sung in his room.

"When it had been sung, he said, 'What devout

words are these!' And he repeated to himself this
verse, ruminating upon it,—'What, sick one, could
she have possessed, if she had not received it, if the
Physician had not been present.'"

1. PRAISE be to Thee, O CHRIST, the CREA-
   TOR, the REDEEMER, and the SA-
   VIOUR

2. Of the heaven, the earth, the sea, angels,
   and men.

3. Whom alone we confess to be GOD and Man.

4. Who didst come that Thou mightest save
   sinners,

5. Without sin assuming the likeness of sin.

6. From the number of which sinners as Thou
   didst visit the Canaanitish woman, as
   also Mary Magdalene.

7. At the same table of the Divine Word,
   Thou didst refresh the one with crumbs,
   the other with drink,

8. In the house of Simon the leper, sitting
   down at the Typical Feast.

9. The Pharisee murmurs, where the woman,
   conscious of her sin, laments.

10. The sinner despiseth his fellow sinner.
    . Thou that knewest no sin, hearest her,
      penitent,—cleansest her, defiled—lovest
      her, that Thou mayest make her fair.

11. She embraceth the feet of the LORD, washeth them with her tears, wipeth them with her hair : by washing, by wiping, by ointment, she anointeth them,—with kisses she encircleth them.

12. These are the banquets which are well-pleasing to Thee, O Wisdom of the FATHER!

13. O Thou born of a Virgin, Who disdainest not to be touched by a woman that was a sinner!

14. Thou wast invited by the Pharisee : Thou wast banqueted by Mary.

15. Much Thou forgivest to her that loved much, and repeated not her sin in time to come.

16. From seven devils Thou cleansest her, by Thy sevenfold Spirit.

17. From the dead Thou didst grant her to see Thee again before the others.

18. By her, O CHRIST, Thou signifiest Thy proselyte Church; whom albeit alien-born, Thou callest to the table of Thy sons.

19. Whom at the feast of the law and grace, the pride of the Pharisees contemns, the leprosy of heresy vexes.

20. What she is Thou knowest; she toucheth
    Thee because she is a sinner, because she
    is a desirer of pardon.
21. What, sick one, could she have possessed,
    if she had not received it, if the Phy-
    sician had not been present?
22. King of kings, rich unto all, save us; Thou
    that wipest away all the crimes of sin-
    ners, Thou that art the hope and glory
    of Saints.

Coeli enarrant.

Also by Godescalcus. Written for the Festival of
the Division of the Apostles (July 15).

1. THE Heavens declare the glory of the SON
   of GOD, the Incarnate Word, made Heavens from earth.
2. For this glory befitteth that LORD alone
3. Whose Name is the Angel of the Great
   Counsel.
4. This Counsel, the assistance of fallen man,
   is ancient, and profound, and true, made
   known to the Saints alone,
5. When this Angel, made Man of a woman,
   made an immortal out of a mortal; out
   of men, angels; out of earth, heaven.
6. This is the LORD GOD of Hosts, Whose
   angels sent into the earth are the
   Apostles.
7. To whom He exhibited Himself alive after
   His Resurrection by many arguments,
   announcing peace as the victor of death.

8. Peace be unto you, saith He; I am He; fear not; preach the word of CHRIST to every creature, before kings and princes.

9. As the FATHER hath sent Me, even so send I you into the world; be ye therefore prudent as serpents, be ye harmless as doves.

10. Hence Peter, Prince of Apostles, visited Rome; Paul, Greece, preaching grace everywhere : hence these twelve chiefs in the four quarters of the world, preached as Evangelists the Threefold and the One.

11. Andrew, either James, Philip, Bartholomew, Simon, Thaddeus, John, Thomas, and Matthew, twelve Judges, not divided from unity, but for unity, collected into one those that were divided through the earth :

12. Their sound is gone out into all lands.

13. And their words into the ends of the world.

14. How beautiful are the feet of them that proclaim good tidings,—that preach peace ;

15. That speak thus to them that are redeemed by the Blood of CHRIST : Sion, thy GOD shall reign ;

16. Who made the worlds by the Word;
Which Word was for us, in the end of
the world, made Flesh :

17. This Word Which we preach, CHRIST crucified, Who liveth and reigneth, GOD in
heaven.

18. These are the Heavens in which, O CHRIST,
Thou inhabitest; in whose words Thou
thunderest; in whose deeds Thou light-
enest; in whose grace Thou sendest Thy
dew :

19. To these Thou hast said : Drop down, O
ye heavens, from above, and let the
clouds rain the Just One; let the earth
be opened and bud.

20. Raise up a Righteous Branch, Thou Who
causest our earth to bring forth, sowing
it with the seed of Apostolic words :
through whose words grant, O LORD,
that we, holding the Word of the FA-
THER, may bring forth fruit to Thee, O
LORD, in patience.

21. These are the Heavens which Thou, Angel
of the great Counsel, inhabitest, Whom
Thou callest not servants, but friends;
to whom Thou tellest all things that
Thou hast heard from the FATHER.

22. By whose Division mayest Thou preserve Thy flock, collected and undivided, and in the bond of peace; that in Thee we may be one, as with the FATHER Thou art One.

23. Have mercy on us, Thou that dwellest in the heavens.

Cantemus cuncti.

THE ALLELUIATIC SEQUENCE.

We shall have another occasion to speak of the "Deposition of Alleluia" at Septuagesima, for which this famous Sequence was written by Godescalcus.

It was first translated by me for the *Hymnal Noted*, —copied thence into the *Sarum Hymnal*, *Hymns Ancient and Modern*, and *Chope's Hymns*,—and, miserably inferior as it is to the original, seems thus to have obtained great popularity. But, most unhappily, those hymnals ignored the glorious melody, contemporaneous with the Sequence. There, for the first time since the words were written, they were, in the accompanying melodies, cramped, tortured, tamed down into a chant, the very kind of music for which the original sense and the English words are least adapted. It is because Mr. Troyte was the author of a chant which, to any one who has heard the original melody, is utterly destructive of the whole prose, that the "Alleluiatic Sequence" is now sometimes called "Troyte's Chant."

If it be said that the original melody is difficult, I can only reply, that I have frequently heard it sung by a choir of children of ages varying from four to fourteen; and never more prettily than when, without any accompaniment at all, in the open fields—the very small ones joining in for the greater part, with the whole of their little energy.

I must confess that it does seem to me unseemly in a great gathering of choirs, such as those at Lichfield and Salisbury, to shrink from a difficulty which can be mastered by an ordinary village choir. The words, mangled by a chant, lose three-fourths of their meaning: the music being so extremely—if I may use the expression—*picturesque*, and the translation having been made expressly and rigidly with reference to it.

1. THE strain upraise of joy and praise, Alleluia.

2. To the glory of their King
Shall the ransom'd people sing   Alleluia.

3. And the Choirs that dwell on high
Shall re-echo through the sky   Alleluia.

4. They through the fields of Paradise that
roam,
The blessed ones, repeat through that bright
home   Alleluia.

5. The planets glitt'ring on their heavenly way,
The shining constellations, join, and say
Alleluia.

6. Ye clouds that onward sweep!
Ye winds on pinions light!
Ye thunders, echoing loud and deep!
Ye lightnings, wildly bright!
In sweet consent unite your   Alleluia.

7. Ye floods and ocean billows!
   Ye storms and winter snow!
   Ye days of cloudless beauty!
   Hoar frost and summer glow!
   Ye groves that wave in spring,
   And glorious forests, sing   Alleluia.
8. First let the birds, with painted plumage
   gay,
   Exalt their great CREATOR'S praise, and say
                                       Alleluia.
9. Then let the beasts of earth, with varying
   strain,
   Join in Creation's Hymn, and cry again
                                       Alleluia.
10. Here let the mountains thunder forth,
   sonorous,   Alleluia.
   There, let the valleys sing in gentler chorus,
                                       Alleluia.
11. Thou jubilant abyss of ocean, cry Alleluia.
   Ye tracts of earth and continents, reply
                                       Alleluia.
12. To GOD, Who all Creation made,
   The frequent hymn be duly paid: Alleluia.
13. This is the strain, the eternal strain, the
   LORD of all things loves: Alleluia.
   This is the song, the heav'nly song, that
   CHRIST Himself approves: Alleluia.

14. Wherefore we sing, both heart and voice
　　awaking,　　　　　　　　　Alleluia.
And children's voices echo, answer making,
　　　　　　　　　　　　　Alleluia.
15. Now from all men be out-pour'd
Alleluia to the LORD;
With Alleluia evermore
The SON and SPIRIT we adore.
16. Praise be done to the THREE in ONE.
　　Alleluia! Alleluia! Alleluia! Alleluia!

Lauda, Mater Ecclesia.

This Hymn, for S. Mary Magdalene's day, was the composition of S. Odo of Cluny, one of the brightest lights of that great Monastery. It found its way into the York Breviary. The variation of rhyme occurs in the original.

EXALT, O mother Church, to-day
The clemency of CHRIST thy LORD;
By sevenfold grace Who wipes away
The guilt of sevenfold crimes abhorred.

Sister of Lazarus that was dead,
She, that in such transgressions fell,
To the bright gates of Life was led
Up from the very jaws of Hell.

The great Physician she pursues,
Bearing the precious ointment cruse:
And by His only word is she
From manifold disease set free.

With heart dissolved in penitence,
And tears that flowed apace, she came,
And piety of deed ;—and thence
She found the cure of sin and shame.

Pardon of guilt hath made her soul
A golden for an earthen bowl :
And for a vessel of disgrace
A precious vessel finds its place.

To CHRIST, arisen from the dead,
And Death's great Conqueror, as she pressed,
His earliest sight she merited
Who loved Him more than all the rest.

To GOD alone be honour paid
For grace so manifold displayed :
Their guilt He pardons who repent,
And gives reward for punishment.   Amen.

[Adapted in one or two recent Hymn Books : also
in the complete edition of *Day Hours of the Church
of England.*]

Chorus Novae Jerusalem.

This Paschal Hymn, the composition of S. Fulbert of Chartres, is not common in continental Breviaries, but was adopted in our own : where it occurs in the First Vespers of Low Sunday.

YE Choirs of New Jerusalem!
To sweet new strains attune your theme ;
The while we keep, from care releas'd,
With sober joy our Paschal Feast.

When CHRIST, Who spake the Dragon's doom,
Rose, Victor-Lion, from the Tomb :
That while with[1] living voice He cries,
The dead of other years might rise.

Engorg'd in former years, their prey
Must Death and Hell restore-to-day :
And many a captive soul, set free,
With JESUS leaves captivity.

Right gloriously He triumphs now,
Worthy to Whom should all things bow;
And, joining heav'n and earth again,
Links in one commonweal the twain.

And we, as these His deeds we sing,
His suppliant soldiers, pray our King,
That in His Palace, bright and vast,
We may keep watch and ward at last.

Long as unending ages run,
To GOD the FATHER laud be done:
To GOD the SON our equal praise,
And GOD the HOLY GHOST, we raise.

Amen.

---

[1] This alluded to the mediæval belief, to which we shall again have occasion to refer, that the lion's whelps are born dead;—but that their father, by roaring over them on the third day, raises them to life.

Audi nos, Rex Christe.

A song of Pilgrims, published by M. du Méril from a MS. of the eleventh century.

O CHRIST, our King, give ear!
O LORD and Maker, hear!
And guide our footsteps lest they stray.

Chorus.

Have mercy on us, LORD :
Have mercy on us, LORD,
And guide our footsteps lest they stray!

O ever Three and One,
Protect our course begun,
And lead us on our holy way!

Thy faithful guardian send,
Thy Angel, who may tend
And bring us to Thy holy seat!

Defend our onward path :
Protect from hostile wrath,
And to our land return our feet !

Thy Right Hand be stretched out,
Thy Left be round about,
In every peril that we meet !

And, O good LORD, at last,
Our many wanderings past,
Give us to see Thy realm of Light !

Glory to GOD on high
Be paid eternally,
And laud, and majesty, and might !
                                        Amen.

Gravi me terrore pulsas, vitae dies ultima.

This awful hymn, the *Dies iræ* of individual life, was written by S. Peter Damiani, Cardinal Bishop of Ostia, the great coadjutor of S. Gregory VII. in his reform of the Church. He lived from 1002 to 1072, and spent the last years of his life in devotion and retirement at his Abbey of S. Croce d'Avellano, having resigned his Cardinalate. His realization of the hour of death is shown, not only by this hymn, but by the Commendatory Prayer, used from his time in the Roman Church, which begins, "To God I commend thee, beloved brother; and to Him Whose creature thou art I commit thee:" originally composed by S. Peter as a letter to a dying friend.

O WHAT terror in thy forethought,
    Ending scene of mortal life!
Heart is sickened, reins are loosened,
    Thrills each nerve, with terror rife,
When the anxious heart depicteth
    All the anguish of the strife!

Who the spectacle can image,—
　How tremendous!—of that day
When, the course of life accomplished,
　From the trammels of her clay
Writhes the soul to be delivered,
　Agonised to pass away!

Sense hath perished, tongue is rigid,
　Eyes are filming o'er in death,
Palpitates the breast, and hoarsely
　Gasps the rattling throat for breath:
Limbs are torpid, lips are pallid,
　Breaking nature quivereth.

All come round him!—cogitation,
　Habit, word, and deed are there!
All, though much and sore he struggle,
　Hover o'er him in the air:
Turn he this way, turn he that way,
　On his inmost soul they glare.

Conscience' self her culprit tortures,
　Gnawing him with pangs unknown:
For that now amendment's season
　Is for ever past and gone,
And that late repentance findeth
　Pardon none for all its moan.

Fleshly lusts of fancied sweetness
  Are converted into gall,
When on brief and bitter pleasure
  Everlasting dolours fall :
Then, what late appeared so mighty,
  Oh ! how infinitely small !

CHRIST, unconquered King of glory !
  Thou my wretched soul relieve
In that most extremest terror
  When the body she must leave :
Let the accuser of the brethren
  O'er me then no power receive !

Let the Prince of darkness vanish
  And Gehenna's legions fly !
Shepherd, Thou Thy sheep, thus ransomed
  To Thy Country lead on high ;
Where for ever in fruition
  I may see Thee eye to eye !

                              Amen.

Crux mundi benedictio.

S. Peter Damiani, in almost all his compositions,
seems to have had his eye on some earlier hymn: in
the present case he clearly follows the *Vexilla Regis*.
The following does not seem to have been publicly
used by the Church.

O CROSS, whereby the earth is blest,
Certain Redemption, Hope, and Rest,
Once as the Tree of Torture known,
Now the bright gate to JESU'S Throne:

On thee the Host was lifted high
Who to Himself drew all men nigh;
Whom this world's Prince in malice sought,
And in His spotless soul found nought.

The Law that in thy form begins
Blots out the writing of our sins:
Our ancient servitude is o'er
And freedom is restored once more.

Thy savour is more precious far[1]
Then sweetest scents of spices are :
The nectar that from thee distils
The bosom with its fragrance fills.

Thou by Thy Cross, O CHRIST, we pray,
To Life's reward direct our way :
Who of old time upon the Tree
Our Ransom didst vouchsafe to be.

The Unbegotten FATHER'S Praise,
And the begotten SON'S we raise,
And equal laud and glory be,
SPIRIT of Both, for aye to Thee!

                                    Amen.

---

[1] The poet has in his eye the stanza of Fortunatus,
not now used, which was given in the note on p. 8.

Cives Coelestis Patriae.

The ruggedness of the translation is merely a copy of that of the original in the following poem of Marbodus, successively Archdeacon of Angers and Bishop of Rennes, who died in 1125. Its title,—a Prose, clearly proves it to have been intended, if not used, as a sequence in the Mass of some high festival, probably a dedication. The mystical explanation of precious stones is the subject of the good Bishop's poem *de Gemmis*, which seems, in its time, to have obtained a high reputation. The Prose which I here give is certainly not without its beauty; and is a good key to mediæval allusions of a similar kind.

Ye of the heavenly country, sing
The praise and honour of your King,
The raiser to its glorious height
Of that celestial City bright,
In whose fair building stand displayed
The gems for twelve foundations laid.

The deep green hue of JASPER[1] saith
How flourishing the estate of Faith,
Which, in all them that perfect be
Shall never wither utterly,
In whose firm keeping safe we fight
With Satan's wile and Satan's might.

The azure light of SAPPHIRE[2] stone
Resembles that Celestial Throne:
A symbol of each simple heart
That grasps in hope the better part:
Whose life each holy deed combines,
And in the light of virtue shines.

Like fire, though pale in outward show,
CHALCEDONY[3] at length shall glow;
Carried abroad, its radiance streams:
At home, in shade it hides its gleams:
It marks their holiness and grace
Who do good deeds in secret place.

The EMERALD[4] burns, intensely bright,
With radiance of an olive light:
This is the faith that highest shines,
No deed of charity declines,
And seeks no rest, and shuns no strife,
In working out a holy life.

SARDONYX,[5] with its threefold hue,
Sets forth the inner man to view ;
Where dark humility is seen,
And chastity with snow-white sheen,
And scarlet marks his joy to bleed
In Martyrdom, if faith shall need.

The SARDIUS,[6] with its purple red
Sets forth their merits who *have* bled :
The Martyr band, now blest above,
That agonised for JESU's Love :
The sixth foundation, not in vain,
The Cross's Mystery to explain.[7]

The golden coloured CHRYSOLITE[8]
Flashes forth sparkles on the night :
Its mystic hues the life reflect
Of men with perfect wisdom decked,
Who shine, in this dark world, like gold,
Through that Blest SPIRIT Sevenfold.

The sunshine on the sea displays
The watery BERYL's[9] fainter rays :
Of those in this world's wisdom wise
The thoughts and hopes it signifies :
Who long to live more fully blest
With mystic peace of endless rest.

Beyond all gems the TOPAZ[10] rare
Hath value therefore past compare;
It shines, albeit of colour grey,
Clear as a fair ethereal ray:
And notes the part of them that live
The solid life contemplative.

Some Council, decked in purple state
The CHRYSOPRASE[11] doth imitate:
In the fair tint its face that decks
'Tis intertinged with golden specks:
This is the perfect love, that knows
Kindest return to sternest foes.

The azure JACINTH[12] comes between
The brighter and the dimmer sheen:
The ardour of whose varied ray
Is changed with every changing day:
The Angelic Life it brings to view
Attempered with discretion due.

Last in the Holy City set
With hue of glorious violet,
Forth from the AMETHYST[13] are rolled
Sparks crimson-bright, and flames of gold:
The humble heart it signifies
That with its dying Master dies.

These stones, arrayed in goodly row
Set forth the deeds of men below :
The various tints that there have place
The multiplicity of grace.
Who in himself such grace displays
May shine with these in endless rays.

Jerusalem, dear peaceful land !
These for thy twelve foundations stand ;
Blessed and nigh to GOD is he
Who shall be counted worthy thee !
That Guardian slumbereth not, nor sleeps,
Who in His charge thy turrets keeps.

King of the Heavenly City blest !
Grant that Thy servants may have rest,
This changeful life for ever past,
And consort with Thy Saints at last :
That we, with all the choir above,
May sing Thy power and praise Thy Love !
                                        Amen.

---

[1] The twelve foundation stones of the Apocalypse
gave rise, as might be expected, to an infinite variety
of mystical interpretations. Marbodus wrote a short
commentary on the Prose that we are considering,

which will serve as a good explanation of it. His
treatment of the foundation stones is *tropological*;—a
more usual one is *allegorical*, which I will give from
the Commentary of Michael Ayguan on the Psalms.
"Jasper," says the comment of Marbodus, "is the
first foundation of the Church of GOD, and is of a
green colour. Whoever hath it upon him, no phantasm can hurt him. It signifies those who always
hold the Faith of GOD, and never depart from it,—or
wither,—but are always flourishing therein, and fear
not the assaults of the devil." Allegorically, the Jasper, the first foundation stone, which promotes fecun-
dity and causes unity, symbolises the first Article of
the Creed: "*I believe in God the Father Almighty,
Maker of heaven and earth.*"

2 "The Sapphire," says Marbodus, "is of the colour
of the sky. It signifies them that, while they be yet
on earth, set their affections on things above, and
despise things terrestrial: according to that saying,
Our conversation is in Heaven." The reason why, in
the Prose, it is compared to the Throne of GOD, is
clearly that verse in EXODUS: *They saw the God of
Heaven: and under His Feet was as it were the paved
work of a Sapphire stone.* "The Sapphire," says
Ayguan, "which reconciles, heals, consoles, gives
sight, and is the King of Stones, symbolises the second
Article of the Creed: *And in Jesus Christ His Only
Son our Lord.*"

3 "The Chalcedony," Marbodus continues, "while
it is in a house, doth not shine: when under the open
air it glitters brightly: it resists those that would cut
it or scratch it: when heated, either by the sun, or by

rubbing with the finger, it attracts straws. By this they are signified who do their good deeds in secret, as fasting, alms, and the like: according to that saying, *But thou, when thou fastest, &c.* But when such men are compelled to go abroad into the world, then their good works shine before men. But if any seek to flatter them, which is as it were to paint or engrave them, they receive not their vain praises, but manfully resist, and acquiesce not in them. And when heated, either by the Sun, which is Christ, or by the fingers, that is by the gifts of the Holy Ghost, they, by word and example, draw straws, that is sinners, to themselves: and cause them to persevere in good works." "The Chalcedony," says Ayguan, "which is pale, sets forth humility; and so the third Article of the Creed: *Who was conceived by the Holy Ghost; Born of the Virgin Mary.*"

⁴ "The Emerald," is the comment of Marbodus, "is exceeding green, surpassing all gems and herbs in greenness. It is found only in a dry and uninhabitable country. Through the bitterness of its cold, nothing can dwell there but griffins, and one-eyed arimasps that fight with them. By the Emerald we understand those who excel others in the vigour of their faith, and dwell among infidels, who be frigid and arid in love. The griffins, that keep watch over them, be devils, who envy them that have this precious gem of faith, and do their diligence to deprive them thereof. Against these fight the one-eyed arimasps, that is, those who go not two ways, nor have a double heart: nor serve two Lords." Ayguan again: "The Emerald which heals, gives eloquence,

riches, conquest, clears sight, fortifies memory, banishes luxury and sorrow, typifies the Passion of our LORD, which spiritually doth all these things: and therefore that Article of the Creed; *Suffered under Pontius Pilate.*" The beryl of the New Jerusalem is described in two of the most beautiful lines ever written by Prudentius.

Has inter species smaragdina gramine verno
Prata virent, volvitque vagos lux herbida fluctus.

a "The Sardonyx," says Marbodus, " hath three colours: the lowest black, the middle white, the upmost red. And it signifies those who sustain grief of heart for the Name of CHRIST: and are white, that is without guile, within: and yet to themselves appear contemptible, and as it were black,—that is, sinners." Ayguan, after the same description, proceeds: " The lower part, which is black, typifies the sorrow of Good Friday;—the middle part, which is white, the rest of Easter Eve;—and the upmost, which is red, the glory of Easter Day." Thus the whole symbolises the fifth Article (as he reckons it) of the Creed: *Was crucified, dead, and buried: He descended into Hell: the third day He rose again from the dead.*

b "The Sardius," continues our poet, "which is wholly red, signifies the Martyrs, who pour forth their blood for CHRIST." "The Sardius," says Ayguan, " as being a bright stone, setteth forth the joy of the sixth Article of the Creed: *He ascended into Heaven, and sitteth at the right hand of God the Father Almighty.*"

[7] Because the number six is symbolical of our LORD's Passion : since He was crucified at the sixth hour of the sixth day.

[8] "The Chrysolite," Marbodus teaches, "shines as gold, and emits fiery sparkles : it signifies the wise and charitable, who impart to others that which they possess themselves. For wisdom and charity excel other virtues, as gold other metals." Ayguan is more ingenious : "The Chrysolite shines as gold in the day : as fire in the night. By the *day*, the good : by the *gold*, their crown, are represented ; by the *night* the wicked, and by the *fire* their punishment. Hence the stone typifies their final separation, and thus the seventh Article of the Creed : *From thence He shall come to judge the quick and the dead.*"

[9] "The Beryl," according to our author, "shines as water that reflects the sun, and warms the hand that holds it. It signifies those who are frail by nature : but, being enlightened by the Sun of Righteousness, shine with good works, and warm others by the example of their love." Ayguan says : "The Beryl, whose virtue is to cause love, to bestow power, and confer healing, sets forth the eighth Article : *I believe in the* HOLY GHOST."

[10] "The Topaz," says Marbodus, whose commentary in this case does not well agree with his text, "is rare, and therefore precious. It has two colours : one like gold, the other clearer. In clearness it surpasses all gems ; and nothing is more beautiful. It signifies those who love GOD and their neighbour." According to Ayguan, the Topaz, which receives as in a

F

vessel the light of the sun, symbolises that which thus
stores up the rays of the Sun of Righteousness, *the
Holy Catholic Church.*

11 Marbodus: "The Chrysoprasus, which is purple,
with drops of gold, signifies those who pass their life
in tribulation and passion, yet constantly abide in
charity." According to Ayguan, this stone (*a*) shines
like fire: and (*b*) communicates its virtues without
diminishing them: and thus typifies (*a*) *The Communion of Saints :* (*b*) *The Forgiveness of Sins.*

12 "The Jacinth," says Marbodus, "changes its
appearance with that of the sky. It therefore represents those who, like the Apostle, can preach wisdom
among them that are perfect, and yet have milk for
babes in CHRIST. Thus," he observes, " S. Paul was
a Jacinth; for he became all things to all men." Ayguan teaches that the Jacinth has the virtue of invi-
gorating; and therefore is a type of *the Resurrection
of the Body.*

13 The Amethyst, according to Marbodus, is entirely
red, and shoots out rosy flames. Its colour signifies
earthly sufferings; its emissions prayers for those that
cause it. For he says, "it is the virtue of virtues to
pray for persecutors. And we read of few that have
done so: yet there are two in the Old Testament,—
Moses and Samuel: and two in the New,—the LORD
CHRIST and Stephen." Ayguan, affirming the Amethyst to give a clear sight, makes it symbolical of the
Beatific Vision—and thus of *the Life Everlasting.* I
add the French verses of Marbodus on the same sub-

ject, with one or two corrections for the sake of the
rhythm :—

> Ici sunt nomme les duze pieres,
> Ki sunt tenues les plus cheres,
> Jaspe, Saphir, Calcedoine,
> Smaragde, Sarde, e Sardoine,
> Chrisolit, Beril, e Topase,
> Ametiste, Jacint, e Chrysopras :
> De saintes âmes portent figure,
> Ki Deu servent sen poûre.
> Ki Deu voudra servir,
> Cum des pieres cintes clairzur,
> En la Cité Deu sera posé,
> E el fundamente bien alloé,
> En vision de paz reposera,
> En laquel sen fin joïr pourra.

Hora Nobissima.

In the xii. century, the Abbey of Cluny, under its celebrated head, Peter the Venerable,—(he held that dignity from 1122 to 1156,)—was at the very height of monastic reputation. Its glorious church, the most magnificent in France, the fulness and exactness of its ritual, and the multitude of its brethren, raised it to a pitch of fame which, perhaps, no other house ever attained.

At that time, one of its children was Bernard, born at Morlaix, in Bretagne ; but of English parents. He occupied a portion of his leisure by the composition of a poem, *De Contemptu Mundi*, in about three thousand lines. The greater part is a bitter satire on the fearful corruptions of the age.

But, as a contrast to the misery and pollution of earth, the poem opens with a description of the peace and glory of heaven, of such rare beauty, as not easily to be matched by any mediæval composition on the same subject. Dean Trench, in his " *Sacred Latin Poetry*," gave a very beautiful cento of ninety-five lines from the work. Yet it is a mere patchwork— much being transposed as well as cancelled ; so that the editor's own admission that he has adopted " some

prudent omissions," would scarcely give a fair idea of
the liberties which have in reality been taken with it.

From that cento I translated the larger part, in
the first edition of the present book, following the
arrangement of Dean Trench, not of Bernard. The
great popularity which my translation, however inferior to the original, attained, is evinced by the very
numerous hymns compiled from it, which have found
their way into modern collections; so that, in some
shape or other, the Cluniac's verses have become, as
it were, naturalized among us. This led me to think
that a fuller extract from the Latin, and a further
translation into English, might not be unacceptable
to the lovers of sacred poetry.

It was published separately, and, by the kind leave
of the publisher, is now reprinted here.

I have here deviated from my ordinary rule of
adopting the measure of the original:—because our
language, if it could be tortured to any distant re-
semblance of its rhythm, would utterly fail to give
any idea of the majestic sweetness which invests it in
Latin. Its difficulty in that language is such that
Bernard, in a preface, expresses his belief that nothing
but the special inspiration of the SPIRIT of GOD could
have enabled him to employ it through so long a
poem. It is a dactylic hexameter, divided into three
parts, between which a cæsura is inadmissible. The
hexameter has a tailed rhyme, and feminine leonine
rhyme between the two first clauses, thus:

Tunc nova gloria ǀ pectora sobria ǀ clarificabit :
Solvit enigmata ǀ veraque sabbata ǀ continuabit.
Patria luminis, ǀ inscia turbinis, ǀ inscia litis
Cive replebitur, ǀ amplificabitur ǀ Israelitis,

It would be most unthankful, did I not express my
gratitude to God, for the favour He has given some
of the centos made from the poem: but especially
"*Jerusalem the Golden*." It has found a place in
some twenty hymnals; and for the last two years it
has hardly been possible to read any newspaper which
gives prominence to ecclesiastical news, without seeing its employment chronicled at some dedication or
other festival. It is also a great favourite with dis-
senters, and has obtained admission in Roman Catholic services. "And I say this," to quote Bernard's
own preface, "in no wise arrogantly, but with all humility, and therefore boldly." But more thankful still
am I that the Cluniac's verses should have soothed
the dying hours of many of God's servants: the most
striking instance of which I know is related in the
memoir published by Mr. Brownlow under the title,
A little child shall lead them; where he says that the
child of whom he writes, when suffering agonies which
the medical attendants declared to be almost unparal-
leled, would lie without a murmur or motion while
the whole 400 lines were read to him.

I may add that of the various alterations, which, in
different hymnals these verses have received, those in
the Sarum hymnbook appear to me far the worst.

I have so often been asked to what Tune the words
of Bernard may be sung, that I may here mention
that of Mr. Ewing, the earliest written, the best known,
and with children the most popular;—that of my
friend, the Rev. H. L. Jenner, perhaps the most ecclesiastical;—and that of another friend, Mr. Edmund
Sedding, which, to my mind, best expresses the
meaning of the words.

THE world is very evil;[1]
　The times are waxing late:
Be sober and keep vigil;
　The Judge is at the gate:
The Judge That comes in mercy,
　The Judge That comes with might,
To terminate the evil,
　To diadem the right.
When the just and gentle Monarch
　Shall summon from the tomb,
Let man, the guilty, tremble,
　For Man, the GOD, shall doom.
Arise, arise, good Christian,
　Let right to wrong succeed;
Let penitential sorrow
　To heavenly gladness lead;
To the light that hath no evening,
　That knows nor moon nor sun,
The light so new and golden,
　The light that is but one.
And when the Sole-Begotten
　Shall render up once more
The Kingdom to the FATHER
　Whose own it was before,—
Then glory yet unheard of
　Shall shed abroad its ray,
Resolving all enigmas,
　An endless Sabbath-day.

Then, then from his oppressors
  The Hebrew shall go free,
And celebrate in triumph
  The year of Jubilee ;
And the sunlit Land that recks not
  Of tempest nor of fight,
Shall fold within its bosom
  Each happy Israelite :
The Home of fadeless splendour,
  Of flowers that fear no thorn,
Where they shall dwell as children,
  Who here as exiles mourn.
Midst power that knows no limit,
  And wisdom free from bound,
The Beatific Vision
  Shall glad the Saints around :
The peace of all the faithful,
  The calm of all the blest,
Inviolate, unvaried,
  Divinest, sweetest, best.
Yes, peace ! for war is needless,—
  Yes, calm ! for storm is past,—
And goal from finished labour,
  And anchorage at last.
That peace—but who may claim it ?
  The guileless in their way,
Who keep the ranks of battle,
  Who mean the thing they say :

The peace that is for heaven,
  And shall be for the earth :
The palace that re-echos
  With festal song and mirth ;
The garden, breathing spices,
  The paradise on high ;
Grace beautified to glory,
  Unceasing minstrelsy.
There nothing can be feeble,
  There none can ever mourn,
There nothing is divided,
  There nothing can be torn :
'Tis fury, ill, and scandal,
  'Tis peaceless peace below ;
Peace, endless, strifeless, ageless,
  The halls of Syon know.
O happy, holy portion,
  Refection for the blest :
True vision of true beauty,
  Sweet cure of all distrest !
Strive, man, to win that glory ;
  Toil, man, to gain that light ;
Send hope before to grasp it,
  Till hope be lost in sight :
Till JESUS gives the portion
  Those blessed souls to fill,
The insatiate, yet satiate,
  The full, yet craving still.

That fulness and that craving
  Alike are free from pain,
Where thou, midst heavenly citizens,
  A home like theirs shalt gain.
Here is the warlike trumpet:
  There life set free from sin;
When to the last Great Supper
  The faithful shall come in:
When the heavenly net is laden
  With fishes many and great;
So glorious in its fulness,
  Yet so inviolate:
And perfect from unperfected,
  And fall'n from them that stand,
And the sheep-flock from the goat-herd
  Shall part on either hand:
And these shall pass to torment,
  And those shall triumph then;
The new peculiar nation,
  Blest number of blest men.
Jerusalem demands them:
  They paid the price on earth,
And now shall reap the harvest
  In blissfulness and mirth:
The glorious holy people,
  Who evermore relied
Upon their Chief and Father,
  The King, the Crucified:

The sacred ransomed number
  Now bright with endless sheen,
Who made the Cross their watchword
  Of JESUS Nazarene :
Who, fed with heavenly nectar,
  Where soul-like odours play,
Draw out the endless leisure
  Of that long vernal day :
And through the sacred lilies,
  And flowers on every side,
The happy dear-bought people
  Go wandering far and wide.
Their breasts are filled with gladness,
  Their mouths are tun'd to praise,
What time, now safe for ever,
  On former sins they gaze :
The fouler was the error,
  The sadder was the fall,
The ampler are the praises
  Of Him Who pardoned all.
Their one and only anthem,
  The fulness of His love,
Who gives, instead of torment,
  Eternal joys above :
Instead of torment, glory ;
  Instead of death, that life
Wherewith your happy Country,
  True Israelites ! is rife.

Brief life is here our portion ;
  Brief sorrow, short-liv'd care ;
The life that knows no ending,
  The tearless life, is *there.*
O happy retribution !
  Short toil, eternal rest ;
For mortals and for sinners
  A mansion with the blest !
That we should look, poor wand'rers,
  To have our Home on high !
That worms should seek for dwellings
  Beyond the starry sky !
To all one happy guerdon
  Of one celestial grace ;
For all, for all who mourn their fall,
  Is one eternal place :
And martyrdom hath roses
  Upon that heavenly ground :
And white and virgin lilies
  For virgin-souls abound.
There grief is turned to pleasure ;
  Such pleasure, as below
No human voice can utter,
  No human heart can know :
And after fleshly scandal,
  And after this world's night,
And after storm and whirlwind,
  Is calm, and joy, and light.

And now we fight the battle,
  But then shall wear the crown
Of full and everlasting
  And passionless renown:
And now we watch and struggle,
  And now we live in hope,
And Syon, in her anguish,
  With Babylon must cope:
But He Whom now we trust in
  Shall then be seen and known,
And they that know and see Him
  Shall have Him for their own.
The miserable pleasures
  Of the body shall decay:
The bland and flattering struggles
  Of the flesh shall pass away:
And none shall there be jealous;
  And none shall there contend:
Fraud, clamour, guile—what say I?
  All ill, all ill shall end!
And there is David's Fountain,
  And life in fullest glow,
And there the light is golden,
  And milk and honey flow:
The light that hath no evening,
  The health that hath no sore,
The life that hath no ending,
  But lasteth evermore.

There JESUS shall embrace us,
  There JESUS be embraced,—
That spirit's food and sunshine
  Whence earthly love is chas'd.
Amidst the happy chorus,
  A place, however low,
Shall show Him us, and showing,
  Shall satiate evermo.
By hope we struggle onward,
  While here we must be fed,
By milk, as tender infants,
  But there by Living Bread.
The night was full of terror,
  The morn is bright with gladness:
The Cross becomes our harbour,
  And we triumph after sadness:
And JESUS to His true ones
  Brings trophies fair to see:
And JESUS shall be loved, and
  Beheld in Galilee:
Beheld, when morn shall waken,
  And shadows shall decay,
And each true-hearted servant
  Shall shine as doth the day:
And every ear shall hear it;—
  Behold thy King's array:
Behold thy GOD in beauty,
  The Law hath pass'd away!

Yes! GOD my King and Portion,
  In fulness of His grace,
We then shall see for ever,
  And worship face to face.
Then Jacob into Israel,
  From earthlier self estranged,
And Leah into Rahel
  For ever shall be changed:²
Then all the halls of Syon
  For aye shall be complete,
And, in the Land of Beauty,
  All things of beauty meet.
For thee, O dear dear Country!
  Mine eyes their vigils keep;
For very love, beholding
  Thy happy name, they weep:
The mention of thy glory
  Is unction to the breast,
And medicine in sickness,
  And love, and life, and rest.
O one, O onely Mansion!
  O Paradise of Joy!
Where tears are ever banished,
  And smiles have no alloy;
Beside thy living waters
  All plants are, great and small,
The cedar of the forest,
  The hyssop of the wall:

With jaspers glow thy bulwarks ;[3]
   Thy streets with emeralds blaze ;
The sardius and the topaz
   Unite in thee their rays :
Thine ageless walls are bonded
   With amethyst unpriced :
Thy Saints build up its fabric,
   And the corner-stone is CHRIST.
The Cross is all thy splendour,
   The Crucified thy praise :
His laud and benediction
   Thy ransomed people raise :
JESUS, the Gem of Beauty,
   True GOD and Man, they sing :
The never-failing Garden,
   The ever-golden Ring :
The Door, the Pledge, the Husband,
   The Guardian of His Court :
The Day-star of Salvation,
   The Porter and the Port.
Thou hast no shore, fair ocean !
   Thou hast no time, bright day !
Dear fountain of refreshment
   To pilgrims far away !
Upon the Rock of Ages
   They raise thy holy tower :
Thine is the victor's laurel,
   And thine the golden dower :

Thou feel'st in mystic rapture,
  O Bride that know'st no guile,
The Prince's sweetest kisses,
  The Prince's loveliest smile :
Unfading lilies, bracelets
  Of living pearl thine own ;
The LAMB is ever near thee,
  The Bridegroom thine alone :
The Crown is He to guerdon,
  The Buckler to protect,
And He Himself the Mansion,
  And He the Architect.
The only art thou needest,
  Thanksgiving for thy lot :
The only joy thou seekest,
  The Life where Death is not :
And all thine endless leisure
  In sweetest accents sings,
The ill that was thy merit,—
  The wealth that is thy King's !

JERUSALEM THE GOLDEN,
  WITH MILK AND HONEY BLEST,
BENEATH THY CONTEMPLATION
  SINK HEART AND VOICE OPPRESSED :
I KNOW NOT, O I KNOW NOT,
  WHAT SOCIAL JOYS ARE THERE !

G

WHAT RADIANCY OF GLORY,
  WHAT LIGHT BEYOND COMPARE!

And when I fain would sing them
  My spirit fails and faints,
And vainly would it image
  The assembly of the Saints.

THEY STAND, THOSE HALLS OF SYON,
  CONJUBILANT WITH SONG,
AND BRIGHT WITH MANY AN ANGEL,
  AND ALL THE MARTYR THRONG:
THE PRINCE IS EVER IN THEM;
  THE DAYLIGHT IS SERENE:
THE PASTURES OF THE BLESSED
  ARE DECKED IN GLORIOUS SHEEN.

THERE IS THE THRONE OF DAVID,—
  AND THERE, FROM CARE RELEASED,
THE SONG OF THEM THAT TRIUMPH,
  THE SHOUT OF THEM THAT FEAST;
AND THEY WHO, WITH THEIR LEADER,
  HAVE CONQUERED IN THE FIGHT,
FOR EVER AND FOR EVER
  ARE CLAD IN ROBES OF WHITE!

O holy, placid harp-notes
  Of that eternal hymn!

O sacred, sweet refection,
  And peace of Seraphim!
O thirst, for ever ardent,
  Yet evermore content!
O true, peculiar vision
  Of GOD cunctipotent!
Ye know the many mansions
  For many a glorious name,
And divers retributions
  That divers merits claim:
For midst the constellations
  That deck our earthly sky,
This star than that is brighter,—
  And so it is on high.

Jerusalem the glorious!
  The glory of the Elect!
O dear and future vision
  That eager hearts expect:
Even now by faith I see thee:
  Even here thy walls discern:
To thee my thoughts are kindled,
  And strive and pant and yearn:
Jerusalem the onely,
  That look'st from heaven below,
In thee is all my glory;
  In me is all my woe!

And though my body may not,
 My spirit seeks thee fain,
Till flesh and earth return me
 To earth and flesh again.
O none can tell thy bulwarks,
 How gloriously they rise :
O none can tell thy capitals
 Of beautiful device :
Thy loveliness oppresses
 All human thought and heart :
And none, O peace, O Syon,
 Can sing thee as thou art.
New mansion of new people,
 Whom GOD's own love and light
Promote, increase, make holy,
 Identify, unite.
Thou City of the Angels !
 Thou City of the LORD !
Whose everlasting music
 Is the glorious decachord ![4]
And there the band of Prophets
 United praise ascribes,
And there the twelvefold chorus
 Of Israel's ransomed tribes :
The lily-beds of virgins,
 The roses' martyr-glow,
The cohort of the Fathers
 Who kept the faith below.

And there the Sole-Begotten
  Is LORD in regal state;
He, Judah's mystic Lion,
  He, Lamb Immaculate.
O fields that know no sorrow!
  O state that fears no strife!
O princely bow'rs! O land of flow'rs!
  O realm and home of Life!

Jerusalem, exulting
  On that securest shore,
I hope thee, wish thee, sing thee,
  And love thee evermore!
I ask not for my merit:
  I seek not to deny
My merit is destruction,
  A child of wrath am I:
But yet with Faith I venture
  And Hope upon my way;
For those perennial guerdons
  I labour night and day.
The Best and Dearest FATHER
  Who made me and who saved,
Bore with me in defilement,
  And from defilement laved:
When in His strength I struggle,
  For very joy I leap,

When in my sin I totter,
  I weep, or try to weep :
And grace, sweet grace celestial,
  Shall all its love display,
And David's Royal Fountain
  Purge every sin away.

O mine, my golden Syon !
  O lovelier far than gold !
With laurel-girt battalions,
  And safe victorious fold :
O sweet and blessed Country,
  Shall I ever see thy face ?
O sweet and blessed Country,
  Shall I ever win thy grace ?
I *have* the hope within me
  To comfort and to bless !
Shall I ever win the prize itself ?
  O tell me, tell me, yes !

Exult, O dust and ashes,
  The LORD shall be thy part :
His only, His for ever,
  Thou shalt be, and thou art !
Exult, O dust and ashes !
  The LORD shall be thy part :
His only, His for ever,
  Thou shalt be, and thou art !

[1] I have no hesitation in saying that I look on these verses of Bernard as the most lovely, in the same way that the *Dies Iræ* is the most sublime, and the *Stabat Mater* the most pathetic, of mediæval poems. They are even superior to that glorious hymn on the same subject, the *De Gloriâ et gaudiis Paradisi* of S. Peter Damiani. For the sake of comparison I quote some of the most striking stanzas of the latter, availing myself of the admirable translation of Mr. Wackerbarth :

There nor waxing moon nor waning,
  Sun nor stars in courses bright :
For the LAMB to that glad City
  Shines an everlasting light :
There the daylight beams for ever,
  All unknown are time and night.

For the Saints, in beauty beaming,
  Shine in light and glory pure :
Crowned in triumph's flushing honours
  Joy in unison secure :
And in safety tell their battles
  And their foes' discomfiture.

Freed from every stain of evil,
  All their carnal wars are done :
For the flesh made spiritual
  And the soul agree in one :
Peace unbroken spreads enjoyment,
  Sin and scandal are unknown.

Here they live in endless being :
  Passingness has passed away :

Here they bloom, they thrive, they flourish,
  For decayed is all decay :
Lasting energy hath swallowed
  Darkling death's malignant sway.

Though each one's respective merit
  Hath its varying palm assigned,
Love takes all as his possession,
  Where his power hath all combined :
So that all that each possesses
  All partake in unconfined.

Christ, Thy soldiers' palm of honour,
  Unto this Thy City free
Lead me, when my warfare's girdle
  I shall cast away from me :
A partaker in Thy bounty
  With Thy Blessed ones to be.

Grant me vigour, while I labour
  In the ceaseless battle pressed,
That Thou may'st, the conflict over,
  Grant me everlasting rest :
And I may at length inherit
  Thee my portion ever blest.

With the above it is worth while to compare some of
the concluding stanzas of the Christ's *Triumph after
Death* of Giles Fletcher, who clearly had S. Peter
Damiani's poem in his mind.

Here may the band that now in triumph shines,
And that, before they were invested thus,
In earthly bodies carried heavenly minds,
Pitch round about, in order glorious,

Their sunny tents, and houses luminous,
  All their eternal day in songs employing,
  Joying their end, without end of their joying,
While their Almighty Prince destruction is destroying.

No sorrow now hangs clouding on their brow,
No bloodless malady impales their face,
No age drops on their hair his silver snow,
No nakedness their bodies doth embase,
No poverty themselves and theirs disgrace;
  No fear of death the joy of life devours,
  No unchaste sleep their precious time deflowers,
No loss, no grief, no change, wait on their winged
    hours.

But now their naked bodies scorn the cold,
And from their eyes joy looks, and laughs at pain :
The infant wonders how he came so old,
The old man how he came so young again :
  Where all are rich, and yet no gold they owe ;
  And all are kings, and yet no subjects know ;
All full, and yet no time on food they do bestow.

For things that pass are passed.

Manifestly the *Nam transire transiit* of S. Peter :—as
the wonder of the infant and the old man is simply a
developement of the *Non minuti, non deformes* of
Hildebert.   But in the stanza that follows Fletcher
has the advantage over Bernard, Hildebert, and
Damiani by his sublime allusion to the Beatific Vision.

  In midst of this City Celestial,
  Where the Eternal Temple should have rose,
  Lightened the Idea Beatifical :
  End and beginning of each thing that grows,

Whose self no end, nor yet beginning knows :
That hath no eyes to see, nor ears to hear,
Yet sees and hears, and is all eye, all ear,
That nowhere is contained, and yet is everywhere.

With respect to the poem of Bernard, Mr. Trench
says very well, after referring to the Ode of Casimir's,
Urit me Patria decor, that both "turn upon the same
theme, the heavenly homesickness: but with all the
classical beauty of the Ode, and it is great, who does
not feel that the poor Cluniac monk's is the more
real and deeper utterance? that, despite the strange
form which he has chosen, he is the greater poet?"
—The Ode, however, is well worthy of translation,
and here is an attempt:

It kindles all my soul,
My Country's loveliness!   Those starry choirs
That watch around the pole,
And the moon's tender light, and heavenly fires
Through golden halls that roll.
O chorus of the night!   O planets, sworn
The music of the spheres
To follow!   Lovely watchers, that think scorn
To rest, till day appears!
Me, for celestial homes of glory born,
Why here, oh why so long
Do ye behold an exile from on high?
Here, O ye shining throng,
With lilies spread the mound where I shall lie:
Here let me drop my chain,
And dust to dust returning, cast away
The trammels that remain:
The rest of me shall spring to endless day!

There are two other passages in modern Latin poets
which are well worthy perusal, on a similar subject :
though the principal part of their beauty lying rather
in expression than in thought, I have not considered
it worth while to translate them. I allude to the
fourteenth Elegy of the Third Book of the *Suspiria
animæ amantis* of Herman Hugo : and to the tenth
Elegy of the First Book of Jacobus Zevecotius, which
is entitled, *An Aspiration to the Celestial Country.*

² Leah and Rachel are allegorized in three different
ways by mediæval poets. 1. Of the active and contemplative life : and thence also by an easy transition
to the toil we endure on earth,—and the Eternal Contemplation of GOD's glory in Heaven, as here. So,
again, in a fine but rugged prose in the Nuremberg
Missal for S. Jerome's Day.

> Then, when all carnal strife hath ceased,
> And we from warfare are released,
> O grant us, in that Heavenly Feast,
>   To see Thee as Thou art :
> To Leah give, the battle won,
>   Her Rachel's dearer heart :
> To Martha, when the strife is done,
>   Her Mary's better part.

The parallel symbol of Martha and Mary is, however,
in this sense, far more common : and is even found in
Epitaphs, as in that to Gundreda de Warren, daughter
of William the Conqueror.

> A Martha to the houseless poor, a Mary in her love,
> And though her Martha's part be gone, her Mary's
>   lives above.

Bernard, in the passage we are considering, has a

double propriety in the changes of which he speaks.
Israel, according to S. Augustine's rendering, means,
he that beholds God. Rachel, according to the un-
warrantable mediæval explanation, *that beholds the
Beginning:* i.e. CHRIST. Thus the change spoken of
is from earth to the Beatific Vision:—and has a reference also to the New Name and White Stone of the
Apocalypse.—The second allegory of Leah and Rachel
expounds them of the Synagogue and the Church:—
to this we shall have occasion to allude in a poem of
Adam of S. Victor.—The third makes them to repre-
sent earthly affliction patiently endured, succeeded
by joy. So a contemporary poem on the Martyrdom
of S. Thomas :

> Post Agar ludibrium, Saræ natus datur :
> Post Lyam, ad libitum Jacob uxoratur.

³ It is not without a deep mystical meaning that
these stones are selected by the poet : as the reader
will see by referring to pp. 62—66.

⁴ *Decachord.* With reference to the mystical explanation, which, seeing in the number *ten* a type of per-
fection, understands the "instrument of ten strings"
of the perfect harmony of heaven.

Patris Sapientia, Bonitas Divina.

This is one, and the best, of the many efforts of mediæval poets to recite our LORD's Passion in connexion with the Canonical Hours. It may probably be of the twelfth century.

CIRCLED by His enemies,
    By His own forsaken,
CHRIST the LORD at *Matin* hour
    For our sakes was taken:
Very Wisdom, Very Light,
    Monarch long expected,
In the garden by the Jews
    Bound, reviled, rejected.

See them at the Hour of *Prime*
    Unto Pilate leading
Him 'gainst whom with lying tongues
    Witnesses are pleading.

There with spitting and with shame
  Ill for good they render,
Marring of That Face which gives
  Heaven eternal splendour.

"Crucify Him!" for His Love
  Is their bitter payment,
When they lead Him forth at *Tierce*
  Clad in purple raiment:
And a crown of woven thorns
  On His Head He weareth:
And the Cross to Calvary
  On His Shoulder beareth.

He upon that Cross at *Sexts*
  For man's sake was mounted;
By the passers by reviled,
  With transgressors counted:
Mocking, vinegar and gall
  To His thirst they proffer:
To the Holy LAMB of GOD
  Such the taunt they offer.

At the Hour of *Nones* the strife,
  Long and sharp, was ended:
Gently to His FATHER's Hands
  He His Soul commended;

And a soldier pierced His Side
  With a spear unbidden ;
And earth quaked exceedingly,
  And the Sun was hidden.

When it came to *Vesper* time,
  From the Cross they take Him,
Whose great love to bear such woes
  For our sakes could make Him :
Such a death He underwent,
  Sin's alone Physician,
That of Everlasting Life
  We might have fruition.

At the holy *Compline* tide
  Holy hands array Him
In the garments of the grave,
  Where the mourners lay Him ;
Myrrh and spices have they brought,
  Scripture is completed ;
And by death the Prince of Life
  Death and Hell defeated.

Therefore these Canonical
  Hours my tongue shall ever
In Thy praise, O CHRIST, recite
  With my heart's endeavour :

That the Love which for my sake
Bare such tribulation
In mine own Death-agony
May be my Salvation![1]

---

[1] It is not to be wondered at that the above hymn should have received many applications to S. Mary: for example: one begins,

Mary, Mother of the poor
And their hope unshaken,
Heard about the matin hour
That her Son was taken;
By the Apostolic band
Utterly forsaken, &c.

More worthy of quotation are the following verses of Hildebert's on the same subject: the rudeness of the translation imitates that of the original:

In twice twelve hours the sun goes through the
heaven:
And sacred to the Lord of all are seven.
The first is *Prime*. In this the Sun was placed
On high, and Heaven with all his splendour graced;
In this we praise our King, the world's True Light,
And pray Him to defend from error's night.
Adam at *Tierce* was made: and given the Law:
Tierce the Redeemer's condemnation saw

And the Blest SPIRIT's Advent.   Here we raise,
The Vessels to the Potter, prayer and praise:
That casting off the old, that Adam now
We may put on, in Death Who deigned to bow
As at this very hour: and Heavenly Flame
May purge from sin, and fire with love, our frame.
At *Sexts* man fell: and CHRIST his sentence bore,
And the noon fiend is raging evermore.
Whoe'er thou art, for whom CHRIST deigned to bleed,
Fall on thy knees, and thank Him for the deed:
Pray that the dragon, who in this same hour
Adam destroyed, o'er thee may have no power:
That GOD, at noon for man a Sacrifice,
May shield thee from the flesh, and fiend's surprise.
At *Nones* by Adam Paradise was lost:
CHRIST on the Cross at Nones gave up the ghost,
And visited the faithful, to reveal
His marvellous light in shade.   Thou therefore kneel,
And pray to join their band, and see their LORD
In the bright realms now lost, and now restored.
At *Vesper* tide the moon and stars, displayed
In their bright course, the Firmament arrayed.
For these fair signs we yield their Author praise,
For the cheered darkness and the lovely rays.
At *Vespers*, wretched now, and doomed to ills,
Adam first saw the sunset touch the hills,
And prayed, as darkness gathered in apace,
With horror struck, for GOD's defending grace.
So thou who at the Font hast seen new light,
Pray that thy Sun may never sink in night.
No certain hour hath *Compline:* yet to GOD
Render we thanks for that day's journey trod:

H

Forgiveness ask from grace : from grace request
That Satan with no phantasm break our rest.
O'er earth, at midnight hour, the deluge burst,
The fearful Baptism of its sin accursed :
Moses, exulting, passed the Red Sea wave,
Where Pharaoh and his thousands found their grave :
David arose to Psalms ; at this same tide
Shall the last fire the good and bad divide.
These things of mercy and of judgment teach :
The hymns and prayers of David mercy preach :
That Moses passed in safety, when his foes
Were whelmed like lead, judicial sentence shows.

Coenam cum discipulis.

The following prose is from the Salisbury Missal:
and occurs in the Mass of the Five Wounds. Daniel
found it in the same Mass in a Missal of the Augusti-
nian hermits. In both editions it is exceedingly cor-
rupt. It may safely be referred to the twelfth century.
The very great difficulty of the measure, taken in
connexion with the exquisite simplicity of the original,
(which under any circumstances it would have been
difficult, and in these it is almost impossible to preserve,) made me hesitate as to including it in the present collection. But though much of the melody, and
more, I fear, of the simple fervour may have been
lost, I still think that it may not be without its value
to English readers.

AT the Supper with the Twelve
Thou, O CHRIST, wast seated;
And hadst prophesied Thy Death
Soon to be completed;

And hadst pointed Judas out
By the morsel meted :
And unto Gethsemane,
After, hadst retreated.

Prostrate fell the LORD of all
Where He had proceeded ;
That the cup might pass away
Earnestly He pleaded :
But unto His FATHER's Will
That His Own conceded :
And forthwith a Sweat of Blood
O'er His Members speeded.

After that the Traitor's Kiss
Judas came to proffer :
"Wherefore com'st thou, friend?" the
    LORD
Saith unto the scoffer :
"Thou to Him Whom thou hast sold
Salutation offer ?
Thou, who hadst the price of Blood
From His murderers' coffer ?"

All the weary livelong night
Neither rest nor sleeping :
Armed bands of soldiery
Watch round JESUS keeping :

Priests and Scribes upon His Head .
Foul reproaches heaping :
Who might see the Spotless Lamb,
And refrain from weeping ?

Pilate strives to free the LORD
From the bands that tie Him ;
But the voices of the Jews
More and more defy him ;
And the tumult waxes still
Loud and louder nigh him :
And the people's fiercer cry
Thunders,—" Crucify Him !"

With the soldiers, straitly bound,
Forth the SAVIOUR fareth :
Over all His holy Form
Bleeding Wounds He beareth ;
He a Crown of woven thorns,
King of Glory, weareth :
And each one, with bended knee,
Fresher taunts prepareth.

They Thy mild and tender Flesh,
O Redeemer, baring,
To the column bind Thee fast
For the scourge preparing :

Thus the Ransom of our peace
Cruel stripes are tearing,
As the streams that flow therefrom
Fully are declaring.

After passed He through the street
As the morn grew older :
And the heavy bitter Cross
Bare He on His Shoulder :
Thronged the windows and the doors
Many a rude beholder ;
But He found no comforter
There, and no upholder.

Him, in open sight of men
Manifestly shaming,
To the wind and cold they bare,
Utmost insults framing :
Guiltless, on the Cross they lift
With transgressors naming,
Him, as midmost of the three,
Chief of all proclaiming.

On the wood His Arms are stretched,
And His Hands are riven :
Through the tender Flesh of CHRIST
Mighty nails are driven ;

In like wise His Blessed Feet
Are to torture given,
As the Hands that had so oft
In our battle striven.

Streams of Blood are trickling down
From those holy sources:
Hither! weak and sinful soul!
And renew thy forces:
This the medicine, that shall cure
Terrors and remorses;
This the writing, that for us
Freedom's deed endorses.

Then the LORD exclaimed,—"I thirst!"
(Meet did Scripture make it:)
On a reed they raise the sponge
To the lips that spake it:
Vinegar and gall they give
To His thirst to slake it:
Which when He had tasted of,
He refused to take it.

Jesu, wondrous to the last!
What was Thine intention?
Thou wast silent of the Cross,
But of thirst mad'st mention:

Not that this Thou feltest more
Than that bitter tension :
But that thirst Thou wouldst express
For lost man's invention.

Calling on Thy FATHER's Name
Thy last breath was spended :
And Thy Spirit in His Hands
Gently was commended :
With a loud and mighty cry
Then Thy Head was bended :
And the work, that brought Thee down,
Of Salvation ended.

But by heart and thought of man
That is past conceiving
How the Virgin Mother's soul
Inmostly was grieving
When the soldier's bitter lance
That dear Side was cleaving :
Cruel mark upon His frame
Of its passage leaving.

That blest form could feel no more
Whence had life departed :
'Twas the Mother's anguished soul
'Neath the Wound that smarted :

When she marked how through His Side
That sharp lance was darted ;
And the streams of Water thence
And of Blood that started.

Wherefore, sinner, haste to these
Fountains of salvation :
Life thou mayest draw therefrom
And illumination :
Cure thou mayest find for sin,
Strength to meet temptation :
Refuge may'st thou gain against
Satan's condemnation.

Jucundare, plebs fidelis.

We now come to Adam of S. Victor, the greatest of mediæval poets. He was born in *Britannia*:
whether *Major Britannia*, (our Island,) or *Minor*,
(Bretagne,) cannot now be known. Of course an
Englishman sees, in his celebration of S. Thomas of
Canterbury, an argument for that which he wishes to
believe.

The school of the Abbey of S. Victor at Paris, produced three of the greatest men of that marvellous
twelfth century, Hugh, Adam, Richard.

> Hi tres canonici, licet absint canonizati,
> Mente piâ dici possunt tamen esse beati.

So says William of S. Lo.

It was probably in the year 1192 that Adam went,
though not canonized, to the glory of the saints.

Till within the last few years his Sequences were
believed to be in number 37 or 38. M. Gautier, who, in
1858, published an edition of the whole poetical works
of this marvellous poet, has given us more than

a hundred; some[1] of them published for the first
time.

Nothing can be more striking, nothing can be more
true, than Dean Trench's estimate of Adam : *if it have
a fault*, I think that it hardly does this wonderful
poet justice.

"His profound acquaintance with the whole circle
of the theology of his time, and eminently with its
exposition of Scripture,—the abundant and admirable
use which he makes of it, delivering as he thus does his
poems from the merely *subjective* cast of those, beautiful as they are, of S. Bernard,—the exquisite art
and variety with which for the most part his verse is
managed and his rhymes disposed—their rich melody
multiplying and ever deepening at the close—the
strength which often he concentrates into a single
line—his skill in conducting a narration—and most
of all, the evident nearness of the things which he
celebrates to his own heart of hearts—all these, and
other excellencies, render him, as far as my judgment
goes, the foremost among the sacred Latin poets of
the middle ages."

CHILDREN of a Heavenly FATHER,
Faithful people, joy, the rather
That the Prophet's lore ye gather,
 From Ezekiel's Vision draw :
John that Prophet's witness sharing,
In the Apocalypse declaring,
"This I write, true record bearing
 Of the things I truly saw."

Round the Throne, 'midst Angel natures[2]
Stand four holy Living Creatures,
Whose diversity of features
  Maketh good the Seer's plan:
This an Eagle's visage knoweth:
That a Lion's image showeth:
Scripture on the rest bestoweth
  The twain forms of Ox and Man.

These are they, the symbols mystic
Of the forms Evangelistic,
Who the Church, with streams majestic,
  Irrigate from sea to sea:
Matthew first, and Mark the second:
Luke with these is rightly reckoned:
And the loved Apostle, beckoned
  From his nets and Zebedee.

Matthew's form the man supplieth,
For that thus he testifieth
Of the LORD, that none denieth
  Him to spring from man He made;
Luke's the ox, in form propitial,
As a creature sacrificial,
For that he the rites judicial
  Of Mosaic law displayed.

Mark the wilds as lion shaketh,
And the desert hearing quaketh,
Preparation while he maketh
    That the heart with GOD be right :
John, love's double² wing devising,
Earth on eagle plumes despising,
To his GOD and LORD uprising
    Soars away in purer light.

Symbols quadriform uniting
They of CHRIST are thus inditing ;
Quadriform His acts, which writing
    They produce before our eyes :
Man,—Whose birth man's law obeyeth :
Ox,—Whom victim's passion slayeth :
Lion,—when on death He preyeth :
    Eagle,—soaring to the skies.

These the creature forms ethereal
Round the Majesty imperial
Seen by prophets ; but material
    Difference 'twixt the visions springs :
Wheels are rolling,—wings are flying,—⁴
Scripture lore this signifying ;—
Step with step, as wheels, complying,
    Contemplation by the wings.

Paradise is satiated,[5]
Blossoms, thrives, is fœcundated,
With the waters irrigated
   From these rills that aye proceed :
CHRIST the fountain, they the river,
CHRIST the source, and they the giver
Of the streams that they deliver
   To supply His people's need.

In these streams our souls bedewing,
That more fully we ensuing
Thirst of goodness and renewing,
   Thirst more fully may allay :
We their holy doctrine follow
From the gulf that gapes to swallow,
And from pleasures vain and hollow
   To the joys of heavenly Day.

----

[1] *Some*—but not so many as the editor thinks. For
the sake of English hymnology, I am bound to claim
the previous publication, either in the *Hymni et Se-*
quentiæ Medii Ævi, or in the *Sequentiæ Ineditæ* of

the Ecclesiologist, of the following, of each of which
M. Gautier simply says, *Cette prose est inédite.*

Vol. I. p. 68. Salve, dies dierum gloria.
74. Sextâ passus feriâ.
101. Postquam hostem et inferna.
168. Rex Salomon fecit templum.
Vol. II. 105. Lætabundi jubilemus.
297. Per unius casum grani.

It was, of course, by the most pardonable fault, a
fault rendered sometimes almost unavoidable through
the international difficulties of obtaining books, that
the Editor made the mistake which I have now pointed
out.

² The Evangelistic Symbols offered, as might be expected, a favourite theme to mediæval poets. Adam
of S. Victor has himself another sequence on the same
subject. It is no part of my design to dwell on the
different adaptations of these symbols; how the lion
is given to S. John, and S. Luke, and S. Matthew: the
man and the eagle to S. Mark, &c. I quote some of
the verses of the Christian poets on the subject.

Juvencus,—if the lines are indeed his,—

Matthew of virtue's path is wont to tell,
And gives the just man laws for living well.
Mark loves to hover 'twixt the earth and sky
In vehement flight, as eagle from on high.
The LORD's Blest Passion Luke more fully writes,
And, named the ox, of priestly deeds indites.
John, as a lion, furious for the strife,
Thunders the mysteries of Eternal Life.

S. Mark's flying between the earth and sky is ex-

plained by the gloss thus ;—that he neither describes
the temporal nativity of our LORD,—represented by
earth,—nor His eternal generation, symbolised by
heaven ;—but, so to speak, avoids both.

Sedulius, a hundred years later, after speaking of
our LORD's true manhood, says :

> This Matthew writes, and thence the human face :
> Mark roars a lion in a desert place ;
> While priestly Luke the ox for symbol names,
> And John, who towers to heaven, the eagle claims.

Later poets carried out,—as we shall see that Adam
does,—the symbolism still further, and made the LORD
to be in Himself all that His servants were separately.
Thus a mediæval epigram :

> Luke is the ox,—Mark lion,—eagle John,—
> Matthew the man : but GOD is all in one.
> The Man in birth, the Ox in death, to rise
> The Lion,—and the Eagle seek the skies.

Hildebert of Mans, after going through these symbols, adduces another :

> The fountain yet distils : increase thy store :
> Each righteous man contains these symbols four.
> For human sense he claims the human face :
> The ox in self-denial finds a place :
> Lion is he, as conqueror in hard straits :
> Eagle, for oft he seeks the heavenly gates.

³ That is, of love to GOD, and love to his neighbour.

⁴ The poet compares the visions of Ezekiel and S.
John. The wheels of the Prophet, which roll along
the earth, signify the account given by the Evangelists

of the earthly Life of our LORD : the wings of the Apostles set forth their knowledge of His Eternal Deity. And again : as four wheels must necessarily keep time together, so there is the most perfect concord between the narrations of the Evangelists.

⁵ The river that was parted, and became into four heads, is explained of CHRIST, the various acts of Whose Life on earth are divided between the four Evangelists. Mediæval symbolism represents S. Matthew by Gihon, S. Mark by Tigris, S. Luke by Euphrates, and S. John by Pison.

1

Ecce dies celebris.

This is another prose of Adam of S. Victor, composed
for Easter.

HAIL the much-remembered Day!
Night from morning flies away,
    Life the chains of death hath burst :
Gladness, welcome! grief, begone!
Greater glory draweth on
    Than confusion at the first.
Flies the shadowy from the true :
Flies the ancient from the new :
    Comfort hath each tear dispersed.

Hail our Pascha, That wast dead!
What preceded in the Head
    That each member hopes to gain ;
CHRIST, our newer Pascha now,
Late in death content to bow
    When the spotless LAMB was slain.

CHRIST the prey hath here unbound
From the foe that girt us round :[1]
Tale, in Samson's prowess found
    When the lion-form he slew :[2]
David, in His Father's cause,
From the lion's hungry jaws
And the bear's devouring paws
    Hath set free His flock anew.

Samson thousands slew by dying :
CHRIST, true Samson, typifying,[3]
    Who by death o'ercame His foes :
Samson, by interpretation,
Is *their sunlight* : Our Salvation
Thus hath brought illumination
    To the Elect on whom He rose.

From the Cross's pole[4] of glory
Flows the must of ancient story
    In the Church's wine-vat stored :
From the press, now trodden duly,
Gentile first-fruits gathered newly
    Drink the precious liquor poured.

Sackcloth, worn with foul abuses,[5]
Passes on to royal uses ;

Grace in that garb at length we see,
The Flesh hath conquered misery.
They, by whom their monarch perished
Lost the kingdom, that they cherished,
And for a sign and wonder[1] Cain
Is set, who never shall be slain.

Reprobated and rejected
Was this Stone that, now elected,
For a Trophy stands erected
    And a precious Cornerstone:
Sin's, not Nature's, termination,
He creates a new Creation,
And, Himself their colligation,
    Binds two peoples into one.

Give we glory to the Head,
O'er the members love be shed!

---

[1] This allusion is not very clear. There seems to be a reference to Saul, in the wilderness of Maon, when, having compassed David and his men round, he was only prevented from destroying them by the intelligence that the Philistines had invaded the land. The thought of the Philistines introduces the great destroyer of the Philistines—Samson.

[2] The victory of Samson over the lion is spiritualised in an infinity of ways. Samson overcame him without telling his father and his mother. From the eater came forth meat, as from death came forth life, or, otherwise, as from the death of the Lion of the Tribe of Judah came forth the spiritual honey which satisfies His people.

[3] As the dead which Samson slew in his death were more than they whom he slew in his life,—so not till after our LORD's death did the thousands of converts fall to the Church. *Samson*, according to the ungrammatical interpretation of the Fathers, means *their sun*: that is, the sun of those that belong to him.—Thus, CHRIST, though the Sun of all, yet shall bring final salvation to the Elect alone.

[4] The reference is to the Pole, on which the two spies carried the bunch of grapes. The pole is the Cross:—the bunch typifies the LORD, as the True Vine; the spies, the Jews and Gentiles respectively. The spy that went first, turned his back on the bunch; thus the Jews, first called, rejected our LORD. He that came last, kept his eyes on it;—thus the Gentiles, though last called, accepted the offered salvation.

[5] The poet refers partly to the Psalm, "Thou hast put off my sackcloth, and girded me with gladness," —partly to the story of the Gibeonites,—by means of whose old sacks, when received by the princes, their salvation was effected. The Sackcloth is here the Flesh of CHRIST; and the Royal Uses, Its immortality of glory after His Death.

[6] The Vulgate is here followed: "The LORD set Cain for a sign."

Zyma ƀetus erpurgetur.

Another Easter Sequence of Adam of S. Victor.

PURGE we out the ancient leaven,
That the feast of earth and Heaven
   We may celebrate aright:
On to-day our hope stands founded:
Moses teacheth how unbounded
   Is its virtue and its might.

This day Egypt's treasures spoiled
And the Hebrews freed that toiled,
   Pressed with bondage and in chains:
From the mortar, brick, and stubble
Heaviest toil and sorest trouble
   Had they known in Zoan's plains.

Now the voice of exultation,
Now the triumph of salvation
  Free and wide its tidings flings :
This is the day the LORD hath made : the day
That bids our sin and sorrow flee away,
  Life and light and health that brings.

In the Law the types lay shaded :
In the promised End they faded,
  CHRIST, Who all things consummates ;
CHRIST, Whose Blood aside hath turned
That devouring sword which burned,
  Waving wide, at Eden's gates.

Yea, that child,[1] our Mystic Laughter,
For whose sake the ram fell after,
  Signifies the Joy of Life ;
Joseph from the prison goeth :
CHRIST, by Resurrection, showeth
  He hath conquered in the strife.

He the Dragon that, devouring
Pharaoh's dragons,[2] rose o'erpowering
  All their malice and their might ;
He the Serpent set on high
That the people might not die
  From the fiery serpents' bite.

He, the Hook, that hid awhile,[3]
Pierced Leviathan with guile :
   He the Child that laid His hand[4]
On the cockatrice's den :
That the ancient lord of men
   Might avoid the ransomed land.

They, whose scorn the Seer offended[5]
As to Bethel he ascended,
   Feel the Bald-head's wrath, and flee :
David, after madness feigned,[6]
Scapegoat, now no more detained,
   Ritual sparrow, all go free.

Alien wedlock first despising,
With a jawbone Samson rising
   Thousand Philistines hath slain :
Then in Gaza as he tarried,
Forth her brazen gates he carried
   To the mountain from the plain.

Sleeping first the sleep of mortals
Judah's Lion thus the portals
   Of the grave hath borne away :
While the FATHER's voice resounded,[7]
He, with majesty unbounded,
   Sought our Mother's courts of day.

Jonah, by the tempest followed,
Whom the whale of old time swallowed,
Type of our True Jonah giving,
Three days pass'd, is rendered living
    From that dark and narrow space.
Now the myrrh of Cyprus groweth,³
Widelier spreadeth, sweetlier bloweth;
Law its withered blossoms throweth
    That the Church may take their place.

Death and life have striven newly;
JESUS CHRIST hath risen truly;
And with CHRIST ascended duly
    Many a witness that He lives:
Dawn of newness, happy morrow
Wipes away our eve of sorrow:
Since from death our life we borrow,
    Brightest joy the season gives.

JESU, Victor, Life, and Head:
JESU, Way Thy people tread;
By Thy death from death released
Call us to the Paschal Feast,
    That with boldness we may come;
Living Water, Bread undying,
Vine, each branch with Life supplying,

Thou must cleanse us, Thou must feed us,
From the Second Death must lead us
Upward to our Heavenly Home!

---

[1] S. Hildebert, following the Fathers: "Isaac, whose name by interpretation is *laughter*, signifies CHRIST. For CHRIST is the joy of man and angels."

[2] So S. Hildebert again: "This Rod, thrown down on the earth and become a serpent, devoured the rods of the Egyptian magicians, because the SON of GOD made flesh, after the dignity of His glory made obedient unto death, by the very means of the death of the flesh deprived the Serpent of his deadly venom, and destroyed death, and the sting of death, according to that saying, ' O Death, I will be thy death! O Hell, I will be thy plagues ! ' "

[3] The reference is to the question, put by GOD to Job,—" Canst thou draw out Leviathan with a hook ?" —But what man was unable to do, that CHRIST could and did effect on the true Leviathan, Satan.—Thus, according to the Fathers, our LORD's humanity was the bait, His divinity the hook ; Satan, unconsciously swallowing one, was destroyed by the other.   Thus in an Ambrosian Hymn :

What more sublime can be than this,
That very sin should end in bliss !

That perfect love should cast out fear,
And better life from death appear ?
Death should the hook devour amain,
And self in self-made knots enchain ?
The Life of all men should be slain,
That all men's life might rise again ?

So S. Hildebert in his Epigrams (if we may so call them) named *the moral interpretation of Scripture.*

Fisher the FATHER is : this world, the sea ;
CHRIST's Flesh the bait, the Hook His Deity,
The line His generation.   Satan took
The offered bait ; and perished by the hook.

⁴ The poet refers to the mediæval interpretation of Isaiah's prophecy : "The weaned child shall lay his hand on the cockatrice's den."

⁵ According to the mediæval explanation, Elisha, going up to Bethel, was a type of the pilgrimage of CHRIST on the Cross to the True House of GOD : and the bald head of the Prophet typified the SAVIOUR's Crown of Thorns.   The mocking children represented the taunting Jews ; and as there came two she-bears out of the wood, and tare forty and two children of the former, so, after forty-two years, the two savage conquerors, Vespasian and Titus, destroyed Jerusalem.

⁶ David's assumed madness in the court of Achish is here regarded as a symbol of the madness imputed by the Jews to our LORD.   "Many of them said : He hath a devil and is mad ; why hear ye Him ?"   S. Augustine, on Psalm xxxiv., dwells at great length on this type.

7 A reference to the mediæval belief that the whelps of the lion are born dead, and continue so for three days, when their father arouses them by roaring: as we saw in the Hymn of S. Fulbert of Chartres.

8 Canticles i. 14. "My beloved is unto me as a cluster of camphire in the vineyard of Engedi;" or, as the Vulgate reads, "a cluster of Cyprus." In the preceding verse the Church says, "A bundle of myrrh is my Wellbeloved unto me." The myrrh is interpreted of our LORD's death: the wine of His Resurrection. Thus Marbodus, of Rennes, in his metrical explanation of the Song of Solomon;   .

Who, dying, caused my heart one hour of deepest
    gloom,
Is wine of royal cheer, arisen from the tomb.

Verbi vere substantivi.

A Sequence for S. John the Evangelist, first printed by Gautier (vol. ii., p. 241 :) it is here also first translated for this second edition.

THAT substantive WORD, united
To the flesh, and therein plighted
  To a life of misery sore;
Him to be the co-eternal,
John's theology supernal
  Testifieth evermore.

On his Master's bosom lying
Quaffed he thence that fount undying,
  Wisdom's stream, his thirst to sate:
Then became, with touch endearing,
Faith to word, to teaching hearing,
  Mind to GOD, conterminate.

Whence in ecstasy uprising,
Things of carnal sense despising,
  And the clouds of error's night :
On the True Sun's truest vision
Soaring high, with full fruition,
  Fix'd he fast his eagle sight.

Sense is naught, if style it slighteth :
He with style so subtle writeth,
  And with sense so Catholic,
That the WORD's true Incarnation
Never more can meet negation
  From the wile of heretic.

WORD, ineffably creative,
Which with Virtue generative
  All things made at earth's foundation :
That same WORD, from John we gather,
Is not severed from the FATHER
  Save by personal relation.

Him, Whom Matthew, more than other,
Sets forth, fed by spotless Mother,
  Born for pain and woe discloses :
Whom Luke's pen, true ox-horn, showeth
On the Cross whence healing floweth,
  As the serpent raised by Moses :

Him, to Whom from death's dejection
Lion-Mark brings Resurrection,
   Rocks then riving, earth then quaking:
GOD of GOD, of Splendour, Splendour:
These the titles John could render,
   Alpha and Omega making.

They relate the earthly passion,
How He died in mortal fashion,
   Crowned with thorns, their suff'ring LORD:
He, upraised to things supernal,
Shows the King of realms eternal,
   And the vengeance of His sword.

On these wings evangelistic
Rolls the Monarch's chariot mystic,
   One among the Living Four:
While the harpers pour their praises,
And the adoring people raises
   Alleluia evermore.

Supernae Matris Gaudia.

This Sequence, to my mind one of the loveliest that
Adam ever wrote, was not in the first edition of the
present book.   I translated it for the *Hymnal Noted*,
whence it has been copied into several hymnals.

THE Church on earth, with answering love,
Echoes her Mother's joys above:
These yearly feast-days she may keep,
And yet for endless festals weep.

In this world's valley, dim and wild,
That Mother must assist the child;
And heavenly guards must pitch their tents,
And range their ranks in our defence.

The world, the flesh, and Satan's rage,
Their differing wars against us wage;
And when their phantom-hosts come on,
The Sabbath of the heart is gone:

This triple league, with fierce dislike,
At holy festivals would strike:
And set the battle in array
To drive their peace from earth away.

And storms confused above us lower
  Of hope and fear, and joy, and woe;
And scarcely ev'n for one half hour
  Is silence in GOD'S House below.

That distant City, oh how blest,
Whose feast-days know nor pause nor rest!
How gladsome is that Palace gate,
Round which nor fear nor sorrow wait!

Nor languor here, nor weary age,
Nor fraud, nor dread of hostile rage;
But one the joy, and one the song,
And one the heart of all the throng!

The Saints whose praise to-day we sing
Are standing now before the Throne,
And face to face behold the King
In all His Majesty made known.

K

In that serene and glorious place
   When this life's many toils are past,
CHRIST, of His Everlasting Grace,
   Grant us to join the Blest at last!
                              Amen.

Interni[1] Festi Gaudia.

A Sequence of Adam's for S. Augustine's Day. I
made two centos from it for the Hymnal Noted.

OUR festal strains to-day reveal
The joys that faithful spirits feel,
As often as the inmost heart
In these true Sabbaths bears a part.

The pure of soul alone have grace
The future joys of Heav'n to trace,
And learn in foretaste sweet and rare
What glories deck the Blessed there :

What bliss, in that celestial land,
They know, the bright Angelic band ;
Who see the King That crowns the fight,
In all His Majesty of light.

Blest is that Country, ever blest,
Which knoweth nought save joy and rest !
Whose citizens for ever raise
The long unbroken swell of praise!

Whom sweetness, more than earthly, fills ;
Who know no grief, and mourn no ills ;
Whom never more can foe alarm,
Nor storm approach to work them harm.

One day of those most glorious rays
Is better than ten thousand days :
Refulgent with celestial light,
And with God's fullest knowledge bright.

This cannot human fancy know,
Nor tongue of men nor Angels shew,
Till endless life the victory brings
That gives for earthly, heavenly things.

Let this our meditation be
Along the vale of misery ;
This occupy each sleeping hour,
And exercise each waking power.

Thus shall we gain, this exile past,
Our Country's Blessed Crown at last ;
Thus in His Glory shall adore
The King of Ages evermore.

The praises that the Blessed know
The Church shall imitate below,
Whene'er she greets, in yearly strain,
The birthdays of her Saints again.

Now, all their battles past and gone,
The Crown of Glory is set on;
For Chastity, as lily white,
For Martyrdom, as ruby bright.

And these beside, a golden chain
Shall Doctors Catholic attain:
Where Angels round their Monarch bow,
Such chain Augustine weareth now.

That we this Saint's blest life may reach,
That we his blessed faith may teach,
May join above, and love below,
The SPIRIT of All Grace bestow!   Amen.

---

[1] Gautier reads *Eterni*: but I understand the poet to mean that the external celebration of the Festival is only the outspoken expression of the internal joy of the heart.

Heri mundus exultabit.

A Sequence for S. Stephen's Day: according to some, Adam's masterpiece. It was not in my first edition.

YESTERDAY, with exultation
Join'd the world in celebration
   Of her promis'd SAVIOUR's birth;
Yesterday the Angel nation
Pour'd the strains of jubilation
   O'er the Monarch born on earth.

But to-day, o'er death victorious,
By His faith and actions glorious,
   By His miracles renown'd,
Dared the Deacon Protomartyr
Earthly life for Heav'n to barter,
   Faithful midst the faithless found.

Forward, champion, in thy quarrel!
Certain of a certain laurel,
  Holy Stephen, persevere!
Perjur'd witnesses confounding,
Satan's Synagogue astounding
  By thy doctrine true and clear.

Lo! in Heaven *thy* Witness liveth:
Bright and faithful proof He giveth
  Of His Martyr's blamelessness:
Thou by name *a Crown* impliest;
Meetly then in pangs thou diest
  For the Crown of Righteousness!

For a crown that fadeth never,
Bear the torturer's brief endeavour;
  Victory waits to end the strife:
Death shall be thy birth's beginning,
And life's losing be the winning
  Of the true and better Life.

Whom the HOLY GHOST endueth,
Whom celestial sight imbueth,
  Stephen penetrates the skies;
There GOD's fullest glory viewing,
There his victor strength renewing,
  For his near reward he sighs.

See, as Jewish foes invade thee,
See how JESUS *stands* to aid thee :
  Stands to guard His champion's death :[1]
Cry that opened Heaven is shown thee :
Cry that JESUS waits to own thee :
  Cry it with thy latest breath !

As the dying Martyr kneeleth,
For his murderers he appealeth,
And his prayer their pardon sealeth,
  For their madness grieving sore ;
Then in CHRIST he sleepeth sweetly,
Who His pattern kept completely,
And with CHRIST he reigneth meetly,
  Martyr first-fruits, evermore ![2]   Amen.

----

[1] Our LORD's *standing* at the right Hand of the
FATHER, here and here only, as a Friend to sympathise,
as a champion to help, is continually dwelt on by
mediæval writers.

  [2] There are four additional, but very poor, verses.

Missus Gabriel de Coelis.

A Sequence of Adam's for the Incarnation. It was
not known to be his till M. Gautier vindicated it to
its proper author. It was not in my first edition.

GABRIEL, from the Heaven descending,
On the faithful WORD attending,
Is in holy converse blending
   With the Virgin full of grace :
That good word and sweet he plighteth
In the bosom where it lighteth,
And for *Eva Ave* writeth,
   Changing Eva's name and race.

At the promise that he sendeth
GOD the Incarnate WORD descendeth ;
Yet no carnal touch offendeth
   Her, the undefiled one.
She, without a father, beareth,
She no bridal union shareth,
And a painless birth declareth
   That she bare the Royal Son.

Tale that wondering search entices!
But believe,—and that suffices;
It is not for man's devices
   Here to pry with gaze unmeet:
High the sign, its place assuming
In the bush, the unconsuming:
Mortal, veil thine eyes presuming,
   Loose thy shoes from off thy feet.

As the rod, by wondrous power,
Moistened not by dew or shower,
Bare the almond and the flower,
   Thus He came, the Virgin's Fruit:
Hail the Fruit, O world, with gladness!
Fruit of joy and not of sadness:
Adam had not lapsed to madness
   Had he tasted of its shoot.

JESUS, kind above all other,
Gentle Child of gentle Mother,
In the stable born our Brother,
   Whom the angelic hosts adore:
He, once cradled in a manger,
Heal our sin and calm our danger;
For our life, to this world stranger,
   Is in peril evermore.   Amen.

Laudes Crucis attollamus.

This Sequence, for the Invention or Exaltation of
the Cross, is perhaps the masterpiece of Adam of
S. Victor.

BE the Cross our theme and story,
We who in the Cross's glory
    Shall exult for evermore.
By the Cross the warrior rises,
By the Cross the foe despises,
    Till he gains the heavenly shore.

    Sweetest praises
    Earth upraises :
    Accents sweetest
    Are the meetest
For the Tree of sweetest cheer :
Life and voice keep well in chorus ;
Then the melody sonorous[1]
    Shall make concord true and clear.

Love be warm, and praise be fervent,
Thou that art the Cross's servant,
 And in that hast rest from strife :
Every kindred, every nation,
Hail the Tree that brings Salvation,
 Tree of Beauty, Tree of Life !

O how glorious, how transcendent
Was this Altar !² how resplendent
 In the life blood of the LAMB !
Of the LAMB Immaculate
That redeemed our ancient state
 From its sin and from its shame.

Ladder this, to sinners given,
Whereby CHRIST, the King of Heaven,
 Drew to Him both friends and foes :
Who its nature hath expended
In its limits comprehended³
 All the world's four quarters knows.

No new Sacraments we mention ;
We devise no fresh invention :
 This religion was of old ;
Wood made sweet the bitter current :⁴
Wood called forth the rushing torrent
 From the smitten rock that rolled.

No salvation for the mansion[5]
Where the Cross in meet expansion
    On the door-post stood not graved :
Where it stood, the midnight blast
Of the avenging Angel passed,
    And the first-born child was saved.

Wood the widow's[6] hands collected,
When salvation unexpected
    Came, the Prophet's mystic boon :
Where the wood of faith is wanted,
There the SPIRIT's oil is scanted,
    And the meal is wasted soon.

Rome beheld each shattered vessel[7]
And Maxentius vainly wrestle
    In the stream against its might :
This procured the bright ovation
O'er the Persian and the Thracian
    When Heraclius won the fight.

Types of old in Scripture hidden
Setting forth the Cross, are bidden,
    In these days, to fuller light ;
Kings[8] are flying, foes are dying,
On the Cross of CHRIST relying
    One a thousand puts to flight.

This its votaries still secureth,
Victory evermore assureth,
Weakness and diseases cureth,
        Triumphs o'er the powers of hell :
Satan's captives liberateth,
Life in sinners renovateth,
All in glory reinstateth
        Who by ancient Adam fell.

Tree, triumphal might possessing,
Earth's salvation, crown, and blessing,
Every other prætergressing
        Both in bloom and bud and flower :
Medicine of the Christian spirit,
Save the just, give sinners merit,
Who dost might for deeds inherit
        Overpassing human power.   Amen.

M. Gautier has printed translations of the fifteenth
century of some fifty of Adam's Sequences. As a
specimen I give the 6th, 7th, and 8th stanzas of the
above.

        Ce n'est pas nouvel sacrament :
        Tel religion nouvelement
            Si n'a pas esté trouvée.

Douche eaue fist qui est amere :
Par li jeta pierre eaue clere
  Quant de Moyse fu hurtée.

Nul salu n'est en la maison,
Se de la Crois n'est par raison,
  Par aucun garnie a l'entrée :
Ne glaive n'a enduré
Ne son enfant adiré
  Cil qui tel chose a ouvrée.

La povre femme qui estoit
En Sarepte, où buche cueilloit,
  Acquist la grace divine :
Qui de la crois n'a creance
L'uile n'a point d'abondance,
  Ni le pot de farine.

¹ This is an idea which Adam frequently, indeed
almost too frequently, expresses.   So in a Sequence
for S. Laurence.

Non discordat os a corde :
Sint concordes hæ tres chordæ,
  Lingua, mens, et actio !

In the Common of Apostles :

Lætâ linguâ mens collaudet ;
Quæ si laude se defraudet
  Fructûs laus est modici.

And in another for the same :

Cui psallant mens et ora :
Mentis mundæ vox sonora
  Hymnus est angelicus.

[2] So we have seen Fortunatus address the Cross :

> Hail, *Altar !* Hail, O Victim! Thee
> Decks now Thy Passion's victory.

The Author of the glorious Ambrosian Hymn, *Ad Cœnam Agni providi*, still more boldly :

> Whose Body hath redeemed our loss,
> Roast on the Altar of the Cross ;

which image is omitted in the Roman recast, *Ad Regias Agni Dapes*. So also Santolius Victorinus :

> Arâ sub illâ, Par Deo,
> Se consecrabat Victimam :

and Adam himself repeats the thought in his second Sequence on the Evangelists.

> Arâ Crucis mansuëtus
> Sic offertur, sicque vetus
> Transit observantia.

So also S. Hildebert : " He on the Altar of the Cross made good the office both of King and Priest : of King, because He fought and conquered, of Priest because He made oblation and appeased : but neither was the oblation which He made, nor the GOD to Whom He offered, alien from Himself."

[3] So Hildebert : " CHRIST therefore willed to be exalted on the Cross, not without a reason : but that, in accordance with the four arms of the Cross, whereby the four parts of the world be signified, He might draw all men to love, to imitate, and to reign together with Him."

[4] The reference is, of course, to the bitter waters of Marah. Daniel unaccountably applies it to the healing the waters of Jericho by Elisha.

[5] Hugh of S. Victor, in his treatise "de proprieta-tibus rerum," under the title "CRUX," says :

"Crux, serpentis ænei palus, ligna Isaac, scala Jacob, virga Moysi, lignum Marath, *Signum Thau in superliminari domus.*" (Compare Ezekiel ix. 4.)

[6] The "two sticks" which the widow of Sarepta was gathering, when Salvation came to her house, are expounded of the two beams which by their inter-section made up the Cross.

[7] I.e., when the bridge of boats broke down under the routed army of Maxentius, who thus perished miserably in the Tiber.

[8] A very clear reference to the Crusades. The two last stanzas are slightly altered from the Translation which Mr. Wackerbarth has given of them, as a se-parate poem. The *Ista suos fortiores* is quoted by Archbishop Harsnett, in a Sermon preached at Paul's Cross.

Quam dilecta tabernacula.

A prose of Adam of S. Victor, for the dedication of
a church.

How lovely and how loved, how full of grace,
The LORD the GOD of Hosts, His dwelling
    place !
       How elect your
       Architecture !
    How serene your walls remain :
       Never moved by,
       Rather proved by
    Wind, and storm, and surge, and rain !

O how glorious those foundations
Which in ancient generations
    Types and shadows half display !
From the side of Adam sleeping
Eve[1] proceeded, figure keeping
    Of a band to last for aye.

Framed of Wood, the Ark effected
Noah's salvation, while directed
 Through the Deluge and upheld :[2]
Called the promise to inherit
Sarah laughs with joy of spirit
 O'er the infant of her eld.

From her pitcher[3] Bethuel's daughter
Giveth Eliezer water,
 And the camels slake their thirst :
For her Bridegroom she prepareth,
While the rings and chains she weareth
 That Himself had sent her first.

Letter held by, spirit scanted,
Saw the Synagogue supplanted,[4]
 Wandering wide, by Jacob's hand :
Leah's tender vision fleeth
Much that clear-eyed Rachel[5] seeth
 Wedded thence in equal band.

By the wayside as she fareth
Tamar[6] twins to Judah beareth
 After many a widowed day :
Here[7] the Royal Maid, revealing
What the rush-ark was concealing,
 Beareth Moses safe away.

Here the LAMB is immolated
Whereby Israel shall be sated,
    Sprinkled with the atoning blood :
Here they pass the Red Sea surges,
While the rising billow urges
    Egypt's host beneath the flood.

Here the urn of manna standeth,
Here the Tables GOD commandeth
    In the Ark of Covenant rest.
Here the ornaments of beauty,
Here the robes of priestly duty,
    . Chief of all the fair long vest.⁸

Here his bride Urias⁹ loses,—
Bathsheba, whom David chooses
    And exalts to share His Throne :
Here in raiment wrought and golden,
Next the King is she beholden,
    As a Royal Princess known.

Hither Sheba's queen proceedeth
As to Solomon she speedeth,
    Seeking Wisdom at his feet :
Black, but comely, she ascendeth,
As when myrrh with incense blendeth
    In a vapour dark but sweet.

She whose glory
Ancient story
Shadowed faintly,
Bright and saintly
Opens here the Day of Grace.
To our Dearest[10]
Lie we nearest,
Resting by Him,
Singing nigh Him,
For the Nuptial comes apace:

The feast, at whose beginning blend
The louder notes that trumpets send,[11]
While gentler psalteries hail the end.
Ten thousand thousand choirs on high
The Bridegroom in one melody
Exalting, sing eternally
Alleluia: Amen.

---

[1] The poet here, after his manner, heaps together
the Old Testament types of the Church. The first of
these is Eve. As she was formed from the side of
her husband while he slept, the Spotless Bride was
formed from the Side of CHRIST while He slept in

death on the Cross. For it was when the spear pierced
His Side that the Sacraments of the Church first
flowed forth.

² Hildebert, in one of his poems, thus expands the
type:—the verses lose nothing by being put into
prose. The Ark of Noah was narrow at the top,
broad at the bottom, and finished about in a cubit.
The beasts were placed lowest; then the men; and
the birds above them. The Ark figures the Church.
Many there are in this who seem irrational as beasts;
—and thence the width of the lower stage.—There
are fewer in it who may properly be called men,
as knowing the things that belong to their peace,
and avoiding sin; hence the comparative narrowness
of the upper stage. There are fewer still who, like
birds, contemn earthly things, and rise to heaven:
whence they are fitly represented as at the top. And
they are finished about in a cubit: for CHRIST is set
forth by the Cubit; and beyond Him the Church seeks
and finds nothing.

³ According to the mediæval allegory,—Isaac is
CHRIST: Rebecca, the Gentile Church: Eliezer, the
Apostles and Doctors whom He sent to betroth that
Church to Himself. The servant's thirst, their ardour
for souls, satisfied by the obedience of the Gentile
converts; as Eliezer's by the pitcher of Rebecca.

⁴ Esau going away to hunt, here represents the
Jew, who while wandering in seeking for the letter
of the Scriptures, and careless about the spirit, lost
the blessing which Jacob obtained.

⁵ Leah and Rachel, as we have already seen, are
usually taken as types of the active and contemplative

life. But they also stand for the Synagogue and
the Church. Leah, tender-eyed, *i.e.* blear-eyed, represents the former, unable to see the Antitype in the
type. Rachel, according to the strange etymology of
Hildebert, signifies, *that sees the Beginning:* i.e.
CHRIST: hence she is called *seeing* Rachel by our
poet, and therefore typifies the Church, who sees her
LORD in the mysteries of the Old Testament.

⁶ Tamar is the Gentile Church :—the garment in
which she sat by the wayside, confession of sins; her
becoming the mother of twins by Judah, while igno-
rant who she was, is explained of that text,—" a
people whom I have not known shall serve Me."

⁷ *Here*, that is, here in the Church, those things
really take place, which, in Scripture history are
allegorically set forth. The Nile is the world, because
it flows through Egypt, the land of darkness. Moses
is the natural state of man; the Ark, his vain endeavour to work out a righteousness of his own :—
Pharaoh's daughter, the Grace of GOD : which finally
makes him by adoption a son of the True King. The
three next allusions are perfectly clear.

⁸ *Poderis.* So Petrus de Rigâ :

Poderis est vestis quæ terræ continet orbem,
   Et caput et corpus præsulis illa tegit.
Sic mens pontificis toti supereminet orbi,
   Moribus ac precibus se populumque regens.
Non aliud splendet nisi veste hyacinthus in istâ,
   Signans quod totus præsul ad astra volet.
Paulus erat totus indutus podere, dicens :
   " Dissolvi cupiens, opto videre Deum."

[9] Uriah sets forth the Jews : Bathsheba, the True Church : David represents CHRIST. Uriah would not go into his house,—nor the Jews enter into the House of Wisdom : Uriah, by too carefully keeping the letters with which he was entrusted, perished ;—the Jews, as we have just been reminded, by clinging too closely to the letter of Scripture, were also lost ;—and CHRIST took the Church from them, and wedded her to Himself.

The symbolical interpretation of the history is very well given by Hildebert, in verses which however are a little too outspoken to be translated.

Bersabee Lex est; Rex David ; Christus Urias ;
  Judæo regi nuda puella placet.
Nuda placet Christo Lex non vestita figuris ;
  Aufert Judæis hanc, sociatque sibi.
Vir non vult intrare domum, nec spiritualem
  Intellectum plebs Israel ingreditur.
Scripta gerit, per scripta perit deceptus Urias ;
  Sic et Judæus scripta sequendo perit.

[10] Jam in lecto cum Dilecto
  Quiescamus et psallamus,
  Adsunt enim nuptiæ.

S. Melito. Nuptiæ sunt Christi et Ecclesiæ ; Dilectus est Christus ; Lectus unitas Ecclesiæ.

[11] According to the usual mediæval allegory,—as for instance explained by Honorius of Autun on the eightieth Psalm,—the trumpets, so usually employed in the Jewish Feasts, are the harsher Law ; the sweeter Psaltery is the gentler teaching of the Gospel.

𝔖tola 𝔎egni laureatus.

A very fine prose of Adam's composition, for the
Common of Apostles :—it was first published by
Gautier. It is now first translated for the new Edi-
tion of my book.

LAURELLED with the stole victorious,
Is the great King's Senate glorious,
  Is the Apostolic Choir :
Heart and lips keep well in chorus,
While the pure soul's strains sonorous
  To angelic hymns aspire.

These earth's highest decoration,
That shall judge each tongue and nation ;
  These the rock of newest grace :
Ere the world was, pre-elected,
By the Architect erected
  In the Church's highest place.

Nazarites of ancient story,
They the Cross's wars and glory
    To the listening world relate :
Thus the Word of GOD adorning,
Night to night, to morning morning,
    " Speech and knowledge" indicate.

They, earth's furthest limits reaching,
CHRIST's most easy burden preaching,
    Propagate the Word of Life :
Earth returns her cultured treasure,
And in more abundant measure
    With the GOD-Man's faith is rife.

Paranymphs of GOD's new graces,
To the New King's dear embraces
    They conduct the Royal Bride :
Spotless, blemishless, eternal,
She, the dread of powers infernal,
    Ever Virgin must abide.

Ever Virgin, pregnant ever,
Youth and age disjoining never,
    From defeat and error free ;
This her bed, truth held sincerely ;
This her birth, faith treasured dearly :
    Grace her dowry endlessly.

These, the temple's sure foundations,
These are they that bind the nations
  Into GOD's great house above :
These the city's pearly portal,
Knitting faith with work immortal,
  Jew and Gentile into love.

  These are they that evermore
  Winnow in the threshing floor,
And from the chaff the wheat divide :
  These are they that came to be
  Oxen of the brazen sea
That Solomon had edified.

Patriarchs twelve in order meetest :
Twelvefold founts of water sweetest :
  Shewbreads of the temple rite :
Gems that deck the priestly vestment ;
Thus they gain their true attestment
  As the people's chiefs in fight.

Let their prayer preserve from error,
Add to faith, and quench the terror
  Of the woe of final doom :
So that, freed from all transgression,
We may enter on possession
  Of the happiness to come.   Amen.

[1] It would be worth while, as an illustration of the above Sequence, to see how the Mediæval Church joined the testimony of the Apostles with that of the Prophets, in the Creed. Every one knows that the twelve clauses of the so-called Apostles' Creed are attributed each to one of the Apostles themselves. The following table gives both type and antitype.

S. Peter . . .	I believe in GOD the FATHER Almighty, Maker of Heaven and earth.
Jeremiah . . .	Thou shalt call Me FATHER, saith the LORD.
S. Andrew . .	And in JESUS CHRIST, His only SON, our LORD.
David	Thou art My SON.
S. James the Greater . .	Who was conceived by the HOLY GHOST, born of the Virgin Mary.
Isaiah	Behold, a Virgin shall conceive and bear a Son.
S. John . . .	He suffered under Pontius Pilate, was crucified, dead, and buried.
Daniel . . .	After threescore and two weeks shall Messiah be cut off.
S. Thomas . .	He descended into hell; the third day He rose again from the dead.
Hosea	O death, I will be thy plagues: O grave, I will be thy destruction.
S. James the Less	He ascended into Heaven, and sitteth on the right Hand of GOD the FATHER Almighty.
Amos	He buildeth His ascensions in heaven.
S. Philip . . .	From thence He shall come to judge the quick and the dead.

Joel . . . . In the valley of Jehoshaphat He shall
judge all nations.

S. Bartholomew I believe in the HOLY GHOST.

Haggai . . . My SPIRIT shall be in the midst of
you.

S. Matthew . . The Holy Catholic Church, the Communion of Saints.

Zephaniah . . This is the rejoicing City that dwell-
eth without care.

S. Simon . . . The remission of sins.

Malachi . . . When ye hate, forgive,[2] saith the
LORD.

S. Jude . . . The resurrection of the body.

Zechariah . . I will raise up thy sons.

S. Matthias . . And the life everlasting. Amen.

Ezekiel . . . When I shall open your sepulchres,
and bring you forth from your
tombs.

Daniel . . . Many of them that sleep in the dust
of the earth shall awake : some to
everlasting life, and some to shame
and everlasting contempt.

[2] *Cum odio habetis, dimittite.* A flagrantly false
translation : the Prophet's real meaning is, " Ye, the
Jews, say, When ye hate *a wife, put her away !*"

In hoc Anni circulo.

The following Christmas Carol is of German origin; and has had at least two popular translations in that language. The earliest begins: *In des Jahres Zirclikeit.* I have omitted three stanzas, as being merely repetitions of the others. The melody and an imitation of the words may be found in the "Christmas Carols" published by Mr. Helmore and myself.

In the ending of the year
Light and life to man appear:
And the Holy Babe is here
    By the Virgin Mary.
For the Word becometh Flesh
    By the Virgin Mary.

What in ancient days was slain,
This day calls to life again:
God is coming here to reign
    By the Virgin Mary.
For the Word becometh Flesh
    By the Virgin Mary.

Adam ate the fruit and died :
But the curse that did betide
All his sons is turned aside
    By the Virgin Mary.
For the Word becometh Flesh
    By the Virgin Mary.

Noe shut the Ark of old,
When the Flood came, as is told :
Us its doors to-day enfold[1]
    By the Virgin Mary.
For the Word becometh Flesh
    By the Virgin Mary.

Every creature of the plain
Owned the guileful serpent's reign :
He this happy day is slain
    By the Virgin Mary.
For the Word becometh Flesh
    By the Virgin Mary.

'Twas the Star the Sun that bore,[2]
Which Salvation should restore ;
But pollution ne'er the more
    Touched the Virgin Mary.
For the Word becometh Flesh
    By the Virgin Mary.

And they circumcise the LORD,
And His Blood for us is poured :
Thus Salvation is restored
  By the Virgin Mary.
For the Word becometh Flesh
  By the Virgin Mary.

In a manger is He laid :
Ox and Ass their worship paid :
Over Him her veil is spread
  By the Virgin Mary.
For the Word becometh Flesh
  By the Virgin Mary.

And the Heavenly Angels' tongue
Glory in the Highest sung :
And the shepherds o'er Him hung
  With the Virgin Mary.
For the Word becometh Flesh
  By the Virgin Mary.

Joseph watches o'er His rest :
Cold and sorrow Him infest :
He, an hungered, seeks the breast
  Of the Virgin Mary.
For the Word becometh Flesh
  By the Virgin Mary.

Wherefore let our choir to-day
Banish sorrow far away,
Singing and exulting aye
    With the Virgin Mary.
For the Word becometh Flesh
    By the Virgin Mary.

---

[1] On this same subject the following lines of S.
Hildebert, which are a good specimen of his rudeness
and epigrammatic terseness, deserve translation.

Two Suns appear to man to-day : one made,
One Maker : one eternal, one to fade.
One the stars' King ; the King of *their* King, one :
This makes,—that bids him make,—the hours to run.
The Sun shines with the True Sun, ray with ray,
Light with light, Day with Him That makes the day.
Day without night, without seed bears she fruit,
Unwedded Mother, Flower without a root.
She than all greater : He the greatest still :
She filled by Him Whose glories all things fill.
That night is almost day, and yields to none,
Wherein GOD flesh, wherein flesh GOD, put on.
The undone is done again ; attuned the jar :
Sun precedes day : the Morn, the morning star.
True Sun, and Very Light, and Very Day :
GOD was that Sun, and GOD its Light and ray.
How bare the Virgin, ask'st thou, GOD and man ?
I know not : but I know GOD all things can.

M

The reader can hardly fail to be reminded of Dr.
Donne, in these compositions of Hildebert.

The reference in the first line is to the increased
length of the days from Christmas, to which the Ecclesiastical poets constantly refer.   So Prudentius :

> Quid est quod arctum circulum
> Sol jam recurrens deserit ?
> Christuäne terris nascitur
> Qui lucis auget tramitem ?

So S. Peter Chrysologus :—"The days begin to
engthen, because CHRIST, the True Day, hath arisen."

S. Notker, also, or one of his followers, in a Christmas sequence :—" This the present shining day testi-
fies ; increased in its length, because the True Sun,
born on earth, hath with the ray of its light dispersed
the darkness."

² The poet is imitating S. Bernard, in the famous
Lætabundus.

☉ Filii et Filiae.

The eight following hymns, the authors of which are unknown, explain themselves. They may all be referred to about the same date; namely, the thirteenth century. The first has more than once been translated: but it seemed to me that its rude simplicity might perhaps be more successfully caught by another effort. It is scarcely possible for any one, not acquainted with the melody, to imagine the jubilant effect. of the triumphant *Alleluia* attached to apparently less important circumstances of the Resurrection: *e.g.,* S. Peter's being outstripped by S. John. It seems to speak of the majesty of that event, the smallest portions of which are worthy to be so chronicled. I have here and there borrowed a line from preceding translations.

ALLELUIA! Alleluia! Alleluia!
Ye sons and daughters of the King
Whom heavenly hosts in glory sing,
To-day the grave hath lost its sting!
     Alleluia.

On that first morning of the week,
Before the day began to break,
They went their buried LORD to seek.
                    Alleluia.

Both Mary, as it came to pass,
And Mary Magdalene it was,
And Mary, wife of Cleophas.
                    Alleluia.

An Angel clad in white was he
That sate and spake unto the three,
"Your LORD is gone to Galilee!"
                    Alleluia.

When John the Apostle heard the fame,
He to the tomb with Peter came:
But in the way outran the same.
                    Alleluia.

That night the Apostles met in fear:
Amidst them came their LORD most dear,
And said, "Peace be unto all here!"
                    Alleluia.

When Didymus had after heard
That JESUS had fulfilled His Word,
He doubted if it were the LORD.
                    Alleluia.

"Thomas, behold My Side," saith He;
"My Hands, My Feet, My Body see:
And doubt not, but believe in Me."
                    Alleluia!

No longer Didymus denied :
He saw the Hands, the Feet, the Side ;
"Thou art my LORD and GOD," he cried.
Alleluia.
Blessed are they that have not seen,
And yet whose faith hath constant been :
In Life Eternal they shall reign.
Alleluia.
On this most holy Day of days,
Be laud and jubilee and praise :
To GOD both hearts and voices raise :
Alleluia.
And we with Holy Church unite,
As is both meet and just and right,
In glory to the King of Light.
Alleluia.

Surrexit Christus hodie.

To-DAY the Victor o'er His foes
For human consolation rose,
   Alleluia.
Who, two days since, through torments ran
To succour miserable man.
   Alleluia.
The holy women to the tomb
With gifts of precious ointment come :
   Alleluia.
And CHRIST the LORD they seek with pain,
For our transgressions Who was slain.
   Alleluia.
An Angel clad in white appears
To bring glad tidings to their ears.
   Alleluia.
"Fear not! O trembling ones!" saith he,
"But go your ways to Galilee!"
   Alleluia.

"Make speed and tell the Apostles this,
That He is risen—the LORD of Bliss!"
　　　　　Alleluia.
To Peter then the King of Heaven
Appeared, and after to the Eleven.
　　　　　Alleluia.
In this our Paschal Joy we raise
To CHRIST the LORD our songs of praise.
　　　　　Alleluia.
To GOD on High all laud give we;
The ever blessed TRINITY!
　　　　　Alleluia!

Finita jam sunt proelia.

ALLELUIA! Alleluia!
Finished is the battle now;
The Crown is on the Victor's brow!
 Hence with sadness,
 Sing with gladness
   Alleluia!

Alleluia! Alleluia!
After sharp death that Him befell,
JESUS CHRIST hath harrowed hell.
 Earth is singing,
 Heaven is ringing,
   Alleluia!

Alleluia! Alleluia!
On the third morning He arose,
Bright with victory o'er His foes.
 Sing we lauding,
 And applauding,
   Alleluia!

Alleluia! Alleluia!
He hath closed Hell's brazen door,
And Heaven is open evermore!
Hence with sadness!
Sing with gladness
Alleluia!

Alleluia! Alleluia!
LORD, by Thy Wounds we call on Thee
So from ill death to set us free,
That our living
Be thanksgiving!
Alleluia!

Jam pulsa cedunt nubila.

THE cloud of night is past away :
Mary, rejoice, rejoice, to-day!   Alleluia.

He That abhorred not thy womb
Hath risen victorious from the tomb. Alleluia.

The dart of death is knapped in twain ;
At JESU's feet death's self lies slain. Alleluia.

In consolation our annoy,
Our sorrow hath his end in joy.   Alleluia.

The Face with spitting marred so late
Is glorious now as Heav'n's own gate. Alleluia.

Graved in His Hands and Feet, the Wounds
Are rivers whence all Grace abounds. Alleluia.

Thy transverse arms, O Cross, are now
The sceptre whereto all things bow.   Alleluia.

Veni, Veni, Emmanuel.

This Advent Hymn is little more than a versification
of some of the Christmas antiphons commonly called
the *O's.*

DRAW nigh, draw nigh, Emmanuel,
And ransom captive Israel,
That mourns in lonely exile here,
Until the Son of GOD appear;
Rejoice! rejoice! Emmanuel
Shall be born for thee, O Israel!

Draw nigh, O Jesse's Rod, draw nigh,
To free us from the enemy;
From Hell's infernal pit to save,
And give us victory o'er the grave.
Rejoice! rejoice! Emmanuel
Shall be born for thee, O Israel!

Draw nigh, Thou Orient, Who shalt cheer
And comfort by Thine Advent here,
And banish far the brooding gloom
Of sinful night and endless doom.
Rejoice! rejoice! Emmanuel
Shall be born for thee, O Israel!

Draw nigh, draw nigh, O David's Key,
The Heavenly Gate will ope to Thee;
Make safe the way that leads on high,
And close the path to misery.
Rejoice! rejoice! Emmanuel
Shall be born for thee, O Israel!

Draw nigh, draw nigh, O LORD of Might,
Who to Thy tribes from Sinai's height
In ancient time didst give the Law,
In cloud and majesty and awe.
Rejoice! rejoice! Emmanuel
Shall be born for thee, O Israel!

[Corrected from the first Edition for the *Hymnal
Noted*; and thence copied, with alterations, in the
Hymns Ancient and Modern, and elsewhere.]

Coelos ascendit hodie.

To-day above the sky He soared, Alleluia.
The King of Glory, Christ the Lord. Alleluia.

He sitteth on the Father's Hand, Alleluia.
And ruleth sky and sea and land. Alleluia.

Now all things have their end foretold, Alleluia.
In holy David's song of old : Alleluia.

My Lord is seated with the Lord, Alleluia.
Upon the Throne of God adored. Alleluia.

In this great triumph of our King, Alleluia.
To God on high all praise we bring. Alleluia.

To Him all thanks and laud give we, Alleluia.
The Ever-Blessed Trinity. Alleluia.

Ecce tempus est vernale.[1]

An Easter sequence, published by Du Méril from
a manuscript of the thirteenth century. The poet
borrows one line from the *Pange lingua* of Fortunatus, and seems, in another place, to copy Adam of
S. Victor. The metre is very rare.

SPRING returns with jubilation,
When the Tree of our salvation,
Chiefest of the forest nation,
Wrought the work of reparation,
    Fallen man redeeming.
Through Judæa's rage infernal
From the nut breaks forth the kernel :[2]
Hangs upon the Cross the Eternal :
Trembles earth : the sun supernal
    Hides in shades his beaming.
Accusation, condemnation,
Pillar, thongs, and flagellation,
Gall and bitter coronation,
This He bore, and reprobation,
    Railing and blaspheming.

Jewish people, crucify Him !
Torture, scourge, and mock, and try Him!
In that precious Blood bedye Him :
That our race is ransomed by Him
  Oh, how little deeming !
Theme of Israelite rejection,
Now, with joyful recollection,
Christians ! hail the Resurrection ;
With good deeds and hearts' affection
  To the Victor teeming !

---

[1] In Du Méril's copy, three lines precede this. But, as they disturb the metre where they stand, and are presently repeated in other words, I take them to be merely a various reading of the third, fourth, and fifth in the finished poem.

[2] Thus Adam of S. Victor compares our LORD's Humanity to the shell ; His Divinity to the kernel.

> CHRIST the nut ; the skin surrounding
> Passion's bitterness expounding,
> And the shell His human frame.
> But in Flesh lay hid the Eternal
> And His Sweetness : and the kernel
> Rightly signifies the same.

Adoro Te Devote, latens Deitas.

The following hymn of S. Thomas Aquinas to the
Holy Eucharist was never in public use in the mediæval Church; but it has been appended, as a private
devotion, to most Missals. It is worthy of notice how
the Angelic Doctor, as if afraid to employ any pomp of
words on approaching so tremendous a Mystery, has
used the very simplest expressions throughout.

HUMBLY I adore Thee, hidden Deity,
Which beneath these figures art concealed from
 me;
Wholly in submission Thee my spirit hails,
For in contemplating Thee it wholly fails.

Taste and touch and vision in Thee are deceived:
But the hearing only may be well believed:
I believe whatever GOD's own SON declared;
Nothing can be truer than Truth's very Word.

On the Cross lay hidden but Thy Deity:
Here is also hidden Thy Humanity:

But in both believing and confessing, LORD,
Ask I what the dying thief of Thee implored.

Though Thy Wounds, like Thomas, I behold
    not now,
Thee my LORD confessing, and my GOD, I bow:
Give me ever stronger faith in Thee above,
Give me ever stronger hope and stronger love.

O most sweet memorial of His death and woe,
Living Bread, Which givest life to man below,
Let my spirit ever eat of Thee and live,
And the blest fruition of Thy sweetness give!

Pelican of Mercy, JESU, LORD and GOD,
Cleanse me, wretched sinner, in Thy Precious
    Blood:
Blood, whereof one drop for humankind out-
    poured
Might from all transgression have the world
    restored.

JESU, Thou, Whom thus veil'd, I must see
    below,
When shall that be given which I long for so,
That at last beholding Thy uncover'd Face,
Thou wouldst satisfy me with Thy fullest grace?

N

Pange lingua gloriosi.[1]

Of the glorious Body telling,
  O my tongue, its mysteries sing;
And the Blood, all price excelling,
  Which for this world's ransoming
In a generous womb once dwelling,
  He shed forth, the Gentiles' King.

Given for us, for us descending
  Of a Virgin to proceed,
Man with man in converse blending
  Scattered He the Gospel seed:
Till His sojourn drew to ending,
  Which He closed in wondrous deed.

At the last Great Supper seated,
  Circled by His brethren's band,
All the Law required, completed
  In the feast its statutes planned,
To the Twelve Himself He meted
  For their food with His own hand.

Word made Flesh, by Word He maketh
  Very Bread His Flesh to be ;
Man in wine CHRIST's Blood partaketh
  And if senses fail to see,
Faith alone the true heart waketh
  To behold the Mystery.

Therefore we, before it bending,
  This great Sacrament adore :
Types and shadows have their ending
  In the new Rite evermore :
Faith, our outward sense amending,
  Maketh good defects before.

Honour, laud, and praise addressing
  To the FATHER and the SON,
Might ascribe we, virtue, blessing,
  And eternal benison :
HOLY GHOST, from Both progressing,
  Equal laud to Thee be done!   Amen.

This hymn contests the second place among those
of the Western Church with the *Vexilla Regis*, the
Stabat Mater, the *Jesu dulcis memoria*, the *Ad Regias
Agni dapes*, the *Ad supernam*, and one or two others,
leaving the *Dies iræ* in its unapproachable glory.   It

has been a bow of Ulysses to translators. The translation above given claims no other merit than an attempt to unite the best portions of the four best translations with which I am acquainted,—Mr. Wackerbarth's, Dr. Pusey's, that of the Leeds book, and Mr. Caswall's, (which last, however, omits the double rhymes.) Chiefly where, as in the first line, and the fourth and fifth verses, all seemed to me to fail, I have ventured another attempt,—possibly to display another failure. In the latter, the two concluding lines, *Præstet fides supplementum Sensuum defectui*, are avoided by all. The versions are: " Faith the senses dark refining Mysteries to comprehend:" " Faith, thine earnest adoration, Passing eye and touch, present." Mr. Caswall's translation, unshackled by rhyme, is nearest; " Faith for all defects supplying, Where the feeble senses fail."

The great *crux* of the translator is the fourth verse. I give all the translations. 1. " GOD the WORD by one word maketh Very Bread His Flesh to be: And whoso that Cup partaketh, Tastes the Fount of Calvary: While the carnal mind forsaketh, Faith receives the Mystery." Here the *incarnation* of the Word, so necessary to the antithesis, is omitted; and so exact a writer as S. Thomas would never have used the expression *by* ONE *word*. 2. " At the Incarnate Word's high bidding, Very Bread to Flesh doth turn: Wine becometh CHRIST's Blood-shedding: And, if sense cannot discern, Guileless spirits, never dreading, May from Faith sufficient learn." Here, the antithesis is utterly lost, by the substitution of *Incarnate* for *made flesh*, and *bidding* for *word*, to say nothing of *Blood-shedding* for *Blood*. 3. " Word

made Flesh! The Bread of nature, Thou by word to
Flesh dost turn: Wine, to Blood of our Creator:
If no sense the work discern, Yet the true heart
proves no traitor: Faith unaided all shall learn."
Here the antithesis is preserved, though at the ex-
pense of the vocative case. And surely S. Thomas, in
an exact dogmatical poem, would not have spoken of
the Blood of our *Creator*. Mr. Caswall, following up
the hint given by the last version, and substituting
the apposite pronoun for the vocative, has given, as
from his freedom of rhyme might be expected, the best
version. "Word made Flesh, the Bread of nature
By a word to Flesh He turns: Wine into His Blood
He changes: What though sense no change discerns,
Only be the heart in earnest, Faith the lesson quickly
learns." In both these last translations, however,
the panem *verum* of S. Thomas is not given; and
Mr. Caswall brings in the worse than unnecessary
article—By *a* word.

Since the first edition of my book, *Hymns Ancient
and Modern* have produced a translation put together
from former ones,—but nearer my own version than
to any other. Their fourth verse is their weakest:—

Word made Flesh, True Bread He maketh
  By His word His Flesh to be:
Wine His Blood; *which whoso taketh
  Must from carnal thoughts be free:*
Faith alone, though sight forsaketh,
  Shows true hearts the Mystery.

It is needless to observe that the Italicised line and a
half is not in the original. *Forsaketh*, too, is scarcely
English. I have substituted an alteration of *Hymns
Ancient and Modern* for my original 5th verse.

Alleluía, dulce carmen.

The Latin Church, as it is well known, forbade, as a
general rule, the use of Alleluia in Septuagesima.
Hence, in more than one ritual, its frequent repeti-
tion on the Saturday before Septuagesima, as if by way
of farewell to its employment. This custom was en-
joined in the German Dioceses by the Council of Aix-
la-Chapelle, in 817: but various reasons render it
probable that the following hymn is not of earlier date
than the thirteenth century. The farewell to Alleluia
in the Mozarabic rite is so lovely that I give it here.
After the *Alleluia Perenne*, the Capitula are as follows:
—" Alleluia in heaven and in earth ; it is perpetuated
in heaven, it is sung in earth. There it resounds
everlastingly : here sweetly. There happily ; here
concordantly. There ineffably ; here earnestly. There
without syllables ; here in musical numbers. There
from the Angels ; here from the people. Which, at
the birth of CHRIST the LORD, not only in heaven but
the earth, did the Angels sing ; while they proclaimed,
Glory to GOD in the highest, and on earth peace to
men of good will." *The Benediction :*—" Let that
Alleluia which is ineffably sung in heaven, be more
efficaciously declared in your praises. Amen. Un-

ceasingly sung by Angels, let it here be uttered bro-
kenly by all faithful people. Amen. That it, as it is
called the praise of GOD, and as it imitates you in
that praise, may cause you to be enrolled as denizens
of the eternal mansion. Amen." *The Lauda*:—
"Thou shalt go, O Alleluia; Thou shalt have a pros-
perous journey, O Alleluia. *R.* And again with joy
thou shalt return to us, O Alleluia. *V.* For in their
hands they shall bear thee up; lest thou hurt thy foot
against a stone. *R.* And again with joy thou shalt
return to us, O Alleluia." So the French Breviaries,
on the second Sunday after Easter, celebrate the
return of Alleluia. After the beautiful lesson from S.
Augustine, in his exposition of the 110th Psalm—
"The days have come for us to sing Alleluia. *Now*
these days come only to pass away, and pass away to
come again, and typify the Day which does not come
and pass away, to which, when we shall have come,
clinging to it, we shall not pass away"—they give for
the responses:—" *V.* Through the streets of Jerusalem, Alleluia shall be sung. Blessed be the LORD
Who hath exalted her. Let His Kingdom be for ever
and ever: Alleluia, Alleluia." " *R.* Alleluia: salvation, and glory, and power to our GOD, for true and
just are His judgments. Let."

ALLELUIA, song of sweetness,
　　Voice of joy, eternal lay:
　Alleluia is the Anthem
　　Of the choirs in Heavenly day,
　Which the Angels sing, abiding
　　In the House of GOD alway.

Alleluia thou resoundest,
  Salem, Mother ever blest;
Alleluias without ending
  Fit yon place of gladsome rest;
Exiles we, by Babel's waters
  Sit in bondage and distress'd.

Alleluia we deserve not
  Here to chant for evermore;
Alleluia our transgressions
  Make us for awhile give o'er;
For the holy time is coming
  Bidding us our sins deplore.

TRINITY of endless glory,
  Hear Thy people as they cry!
Grant us all to keep Thy Easter
  In our Home beyond the sky;
There to Thee our Alleluia
  Singing everlastingly.   Amen.

[Corrected for the *Hymnal Noted*; thence with
alterations in *Hymns Ancient and Modern* and *Sarum*.]

Dies est laetitiae.

A German carol;—at least it does not seem to have
been used in the offices of the Church. It is perhaps
scarcely worth mentioning that Luther believed it
inspired.

ROYAL Day that chasest gloom!
　Day by gladness speeded!
Thou beheld'st from Mary's womb
　How the King proceeded;
Whom, True man, with praise our Choir
Hails, and love, and heart's desire,
　Joy and admiration;
Who, True GOD, enthroned in light,
Passeth wonder, passeth sight,
　Passeth cogitation.

On the Virgin as He hung,
　GOD, the world's Creator,
Like a rose from lily sprung,—
　Stood astounded nature:

That a Maiden's arms enfold
Him That made the world of old,
　Him That ever liveth:
That a Maiden's spotless breast
To the King Eternal rest,
　Warmth and nurture giveth!

As the sunbeam through the glass
　Passeth but not staineth,
Thus the Virgin, as she was,
　Virgin still remaineth: ·
Blessed Mother, in whose womb
· Lay the Light that exiles gloom,
　GOD, the LORD of Ages:
Blessed Maid! from whom the LORD,
Her own Infant, GOD adored,
　Hunger's pangs assuages.

―――――

[See the lovely melody in the "Christmas Carols"
published by Mr. Helmore and myself.]

Nobi partus gaudium.

This sequence, for such it appears, was first published by Du Méril from a MS. of the fourteenth century. The writer was clearly formed in the school of Adam of S. Victor. The metre is very uncommon: and, perhaps, not very pleasing.

LET the faithful raise the lay
To the new-born King to-day :
That the Light of Light would come
From the Virgin's holy womb :
Purging Adam's guilt away,
Shedding joy and scattering gloom.

Long had darkness reigned around :
Light and freedom none were found,
Hope of exit none in ken
For the fallen tribes of men,
Whom the Prince of this world bound
Fast within his doleful den.

From the dungeon and the cave
Had the Law no power to save :
While the wounded traveller lay
Breathing of his soul away,
There the Priest[1] no aidance gave,
Word of hope had none to say.

So the Levite, passing by,
On him cast an idle eye :
For the Law, that sin displayed,
Showed its stain, but gave no aid,
Till to succour her drew nigh,
Grace, with mightier powers arrayed.

Prophet's staff was sent before,
But the child was ne'er the more
Raised to life, until He came
Who had sent afore the same :
GOD and man, whom Mary bore,
Taking of an infant frame.[3]

----

[1] The poet, whether by design or not, misses the usual interpretation of the Fathers : that by the Priest was meant the Patriarchal dispensation, which "passed by on the other side," neither doing, nor professing

to do any thing for the salvation of man; while by the Levite, who " came and looked on" the Traveller, the Law was typified :—which indeed showed man his sinfulness, but gave no effectual help.

[2] The allusion is, of course, to the staff of Elisha. Our LORD's taking the form of a child is here considered as symbolised by the Prophet's stretching himself upon the dead son of the Shunammite, and thus, so to speak, taking his form before raising him to life.

O quam glorificum.

The following is a German hymn, probably of the
early part of the fifteenth century. It was first published by Mone, in his first volume. I have not
retained the double rhyme at the close of each line ;
otherwise the general rule is observed. It was not in
the first edition.

O WHAT the blessedness, dwelling alone,
Filled with the peace to the worldly unknown,
As in a mirror the Bridegroom to see,
Fearing no peril nor toil that can be !

This is a joy that costs trouble and care,
Fleeting, and broken, and utterly rare :
For a long warfare is all of our life,—
Little of peace, and abundance of strife

For that iniquity now hath increased,
Therefore true love waxeth cold, and hath
    ceased :
Sharp contradictions beset us about ;
Faintings within us, and fightings without.

Woe is me! what is existence below?
Trouble on trouble, and blow upon blow!
What is in this world save sorrowful years,
Much tribulation, and plentiful tears?

"Dust of the earth, dost thou wail and repine,
For that, in sundry ways, trial is thine?
Leisure and softness—to these hast thou right?
Draw the sword—grasp the shield—gird thee
    for fight!

"As in the furnace the gold must be proved,
So, by affliction, the son that is loved:
For My true followers trouble is stored;
Nor is the servant above his own LORD.

"Hast thou forgotten the tale thou hast read?
I, when on earth, had no place for My head:
This was the Cross all My life long I bare,
When, the world's Maker, I exiled Me there.

"Thou, the more lowly thou humblest thee
    here,
All the more perfectly shalt be My peer:
I Who am Highest, True GOD of True GOD,
I was the meanest, when this world I trod.

"See how especially all Mine elect
Manifold woes and vexations affect:
Filled with the merit of virtues by this,
Now everlastingly joy they in bliss.

"Wouldst thou but ponder the promise I
      make,
Willingly, joyfully, pain wouldst thou take:
That in My kingdom the joys thou may'st see
Of the Confessors who suffered for Me.

"Nothing more precious than this in My
      sight;
If with thyself and thine own will thou fight:
Bearing all anguish, renouncing all bliss,
And, as a sacrifice, offering this.

"For, if iniquity beareth not sway,
Happy adversity merits alway:
THIS is the Royal road, leading above,
Which My Elect took to kingdoms of love."

Grant Thou this patience, O JESU, to me!
Grant Thou Thy graces, my safeguard to be!
So that in all things Thy will may be mine,
Bearing all troubles, because they are Thine.

Still let me study like Thee to appear,—
Still let me seek to be crucified here :
That, if my anguish, like Thine, is increased,
I may sit also with Thee at Thy Feast.

Low before Him with our praises we fall,
Of Whom, and *through* Whom, and *in* Whom
   are all :
Of Whom,—the FATHER, and *in* Whom,—the
   SON,
Through Whom,—the SPIRIT, with these ever
   One.

                        Amen.

Multi sunt Presbyteri.

The choice quaintness and deep simple piety of the
original have always made the following poem, (which
may be of the end of the fourteenth century,) a grea
favourite with me.   It was first published from a MS.
belonging to the Cathedral of Oehringen, in the
Serapæum, (I. 107,) but very incorrectly.   Edélestand
du Méril printed it from a French MS. : his text is
better, but still very incorrect : and in several places
the author's original draught is given, in addition to his
revised form.   Du Méril has also added to it, as one
and the same poem, the very striking *Dictamen ad
Sacerdotes*, which is affixed to so many mediæval
Breviaries, (among others the *Sarum*.)   A very good
translation of this latter has been published by Hayes.
The two compositions have no further connexion than
that of subject.

In translating it I have taken the liberty of which
Tusser avails himself, regarding the same fowl of
which this poem treats, (as well as in a multitude of
other cases,)—the omission of the article :—

" Cock croweth at midnight, few times above six," &c.

MANY are the Presbyters
  Lacking information
Why the Cock on each church tow'r
  Meetly finds his station ;
Therefore I will now hereof
  Tell the cause and reason,
If ye lend me patient ears
  For a little season.

Cock, he is a marvellous
  Bird of GOD's creating,
Faithfully the Priestly life
  In his ways relating :
Such a life as he must lead
  Who a parish tendeth,
And his flock from jeopardy
  Evermore defendeth.

From what point the wind his course
  On the tower directeth,
To that point the cock his head
  Manfully objecteth :
Thus the Priest, where'er he sees
  Satan warfare waging,
Thither doth he turn himself
  For his flock engaging.

Cock, he, more than other birds
  Way through ether winging,
Heareth high above the clouds
  Choirs Angelic singing ;
Thus he warns us cast away
  Evil word and doing,
Thoughts and joys of things above
  Evermore ensuing.

On his head a royal crown,
  Like a king, he beareth ;
On his foot a shapely spur,
  Like a knight, he weareth ;
Waxeth golden more and more
  As in age he groweth ;
And the lion quakes with fear,
  When by night he croweth.

Thus they spur the idle on,
  On their warfare bowning,
Thus GOD marks His heritage,
  By the tonsure crowning :
As they wax in age, their crowns
  Should but shine more glorious,
And the Lion-foe should quake
  At their shout victorious.

Cock hath soldier's buskins on,
　Strengthening and protecting,
Singularly every fault
　Of his hens correcting :
So the Priest is bound to do,
　Punishing transgression,
Making men in word and deed
　Better by confession.

Cock, he rules a tribe of hens,
　Laws and customs giving,
And hath many cares of heart
　For their way of living :
Even thus parochial cure
　Whoso entertaineth,
Let him learn and let him do
　That which GOD ordaineth.

Cock, he findeth grains of wheat,
　And his hens he calleth,
Giving to the dearer ones
　What to each befalleth :
Midst his people thus the clerk
　Scripture nurture shareth,
And for sick, and poor, and maim'd
　Providently careth.

Cock is speedy, in his hens
　Very sore amercing,
Whom with other than himself
　He may find conversing :
Thus the Priest doth, unto them
　Due correction giving,
From the LORD who turn away
　Unto evil living.

From the egg that cock hath hatch'd
　Basilisk proceedeth ;[1]
From the negligence of Priest
　Satan's increase speedeth ;
If he teach not men to fear
　Punishment infernal,
If he lead not men to look
　Up to joys supernal.

When it draws to vesper-tide,
　Cock neglecteth never,
But he goeth straight to roost,
　With his subjects ever :
So that then, when midnight comes,
　He may well and truly
Call GOD's Priests to rise and sing
　Matin service duly.

[1] Du Méril assures us that this belief, namely,
that a basilisk will proceed from the egg upon which

Cock at midnight croweth loud,
    And in this delighteth ;
But, before he crows, his sides
    With his wings he smiteth :
So the Priest at midnight, when
    Him from rest he raiseth,
Firstly doeth penitence,
    After that he praiseth.

Let the present things suffice
    Of the cock related,
Only in the hearers' hearts
    Let them be located :
This sweet musk, if fully chewed
    In its truth and meetness,
Shall abound with more than all
    Aromatic sweetness.

Thus the cock hath preached to you ;
    Hear with duty fervent,
Priests and Levites of the LORD,
    Every faithful servant !
That at last it may be said,
    " Come to joys supernal :—"
Yea, bestow on all of us,
    FATHER, Life Eternal !

a cock has sat, exists in Normandy to the present
day.

Omnis fidelis gaudeat.

The following Hymn, from the Meissen Breviary, was appropriated to the Feast of the Face of our SAVIOUR, celebrated on January 15. This was one of the festivals which, however well suited to the simplicity of the middle ages, have been, it cannot be denied, wisely allowed to drop from the Calendar. The hymn itself, though exceedingly rude, is, to my mind, of a very sweet simplicity.

LET every faithful heart rejoice,
And render thanks to GOD on high :
And with each power of soul and voice
Extol His praises worthily.

Into this dark world JESUS came,
And all men might His form behold ;
While to the limits of the same
He passed, that we might be consoled.

To all He showed that gentle Face :
On good and bad alike it shone :
Its perfect loveliness and grace
The LORD of all concealed from none.

O love of CHRIST beyond all love !
O clemency beyond all thought !
O grace all praise of men above,
Whereby such gifts to men are brought !

O Blessed Face, whose praise we sing !
Here in the Way we worship Thee :
That in the Country of our King
Filled with Thy glory we may be !

To GOD on High be glory meet !
Equal to Thee, Eternal SON !
Equal to Thee, Blest PARACLETE,
While never-ending ages run !   Amen.

Gloriosi Salvatoris.

A German Hymn on the Festival of the Holy Name of JESUS. All that can be said of its date is, that it is clearly posterior to the *Pange Lingua* of S. Thomas, which it imitates. This hymn has been adopted in several hymnals.

To the Name that brings Salvation
   Honour, worship, laud we pay :
That for many a generation
   Hid in GOD's foreknowledge lay ;
But to every tongue and nation
   Holy Church proclaims to-day.

Name of gladness, Name of pleasure,
   By the tongue ineffable,
Name of sweetness passing measure,
   To the ear delectable,
'Tis our safeguard and our treasure,
   'Tis our help 'gainst sin and hell.

'Tis the Name for adoration,
  'Tis the Name of victory;
'Tis the Name for meditation
  In the vale of misery :
'Tis the Name for veneration
  By the Citizens on high.

'Tis the Name that whoso preaches
  Finds it music in his ear :
'Tis the Name that whoso teaches
  Finds more sweet than honey's cheer :
Who its perfect wisdom reaches
  Makes his ghostly vision clear.

'Tis the Name by right exalted
  Over every other Name :
That when we are sore assaulted
  Puts our enemies to shame :
Strength to them that else had halted,
  Eyes to blind, and feet to lame.

JESU, we Thy Name adoring
  Long to see Thee as Thou art :
Of Thy clemency imploring
  So to write it in our heart,
That, hereafter, upward soaring,
  We with Angels may have part. Amen.

Redeundo per gyrum.

The following Prose, on the Theban Legion, was first published in my Collection of Sequences from a MS. at Wolfenbüttel :—and I never saw it in any other MS. or printed Missal. Mone subsequently edited it from a better MS.: and Daniel, comparing the two, has given a more perfect copy than either. It was not, of course, in the first edition of this book.

As the circling year rolls on
  O'er our northern region,
Comes the day that gave the crown
  To the Theban Legion :
Equinoctial was that day,[1]
  As the world believed it ;
Everlasting was its ray,
  As that band received it.
They had light that knew no end,
  Chiefs of ancient story,
That the sun illumined not,
  But diviner glory ;

Day of calm serenity,
    By no twilight followed—
Day when age was changed to youth,
    Death in victory swallowed.
There Mauritius, spite his name,[2]
    Shines in heavenly whiteness :
Ethiopian Candidus
    Puts on candid brightness :
Exuperius o'er his foes
    There superior standeth ;
Victor, vanquished though by death,[3]
    With the victors bandeth ;
Innocentius meetly falls,
    Innocence defending :
And Vitalis for his meed
    Hath the life unending.
Six the chiefs that led the war,
    Thousands six they guided ;
For the truth they stood in fight,
    Careless what betided :
Though their necks endured the sword,
    They, the gallant hearted,
From their Head—their Head and ours—
    Never could be parted.
Pray, ye valiant six, that we
    Still may bid defiance,
So we gain the six-stepped[4] Throne,
    To the twice six lions :

That the six adversities[5]
  May beset us never,
Pray, ye glorious ones, who now
  Wear the Crown for ever !

----

[1] The Theban Legion is commemorated on Sept. 22. The poet would remind us that the day which, had they remained in the world, would have had as many hours of darkness as of light, was changed for them into the everlasting day of heaven.

[2] The names particularized by the poet are the only six which have come down to us. Of these S. Maurice was the commanding officer; Exuperius, a Senator; Candidus, a Campidoctor, that is, the officer who gave instruction in military exercises; Victor, a veteran; Innocent and Vitalis, simple soldiers.

[3] So the legend of S. Victor of Marseilles tells us that, at the very moment his head was struck off, a voice was heard from heaven, "Thou hast conquered, Blessed Victor, thou hast conquered." And so Adam of S. Victor,

        Victor, effuso sanguine,
        Victoris dignus nomine,
        Cœlo receptus hodie,
        Palmam tenet victoriæ.

⁴ The reference is of course to Solomon's Throne—as the type of that more glorious Throne of the Eternal Solomon :—the lions being the temptations and difficulties which assail us in our progress towards it.

⁵ The poet refers to Job v. 19. Daniel also sees a reference to the six curses addressed to the wicked in our LORD's description of the Day of Judgment.

O beata beatorum. ·

This very elegant sequence is of German origin. Its rhymes are irregular in the original, as here. It was inserted in the Hymnal Noted.

BLESSED Feasts of Blessed Martyrs!
  Saintly days of saintly men!
With affection's recollections
  Greet we your return again.

Mighty deeds they wrought, and wonders,
  While a frame of flesh they bore:
We with meetest praise, and sweetest, ·
  Honour them for evermore.

Faith unblenching, Hope unquenching,
  Well-lov'd LORD, and single heart,—
Thus they glorious and victorious
  Bore the Martyr's happy part.

Blood in slaughter pour'd like water,
  Torments long and heavy chain,
Flame, and axe, and laceration,
  They endur'd, and conquered pain.

While they passed through divers tortures,
  Till they sank by death oppress'd,
Earth's rejected were elected
  To have portion with the Blest.

By contempt of worldly pleasures,
  And by mighty battles done,
They have reached the Land of Angels,
  And with them are knit in one.

They are made co-heirs of glory,
  And they sit with CHRIST on high:
Oh that, as He heard their weeping,
  He may also hear our cry;

Till, this weary life completed,
  And its many labours past,
He shall grant us to be seated
  In our FATHER'S Home at last!   Amen.

Aestimabit Hortolanum.

The very elegant hymn, *Pange lingua Magdalena*,
of English origin, is in the Sarum Breviary divided
into three, for Vespers, Matins, and Lauds. I translated it for the *Hymnal Noted*; but it was thought
too complex for popular use. The Lauds hymn was
accidentally kept: the other translations lost. It is
in the Clewer edition of the Day Hours.

As the Gardener Him addressing,
  Well and rightly she believ'd :
He, the Sower, gave His blessing
  To the seed her heart receiv'd :
Not at first His Form confessing,
  Soon His Voice her soul perceiv'd.

She beheld, as yet not knowing
  In the mystical disguise,
CHRIST, That in her breast was sowing
  Deep and heavenly mysteries :
Till His Voice, her name bestowing,
  Bade her hear and recognize.

She to JESUS, JESUS weepeth,
  Of her LORD removed complains;
JESUS in her breast she keepeth;
  JESUS seeks, yet still retains:
He That soweth, He That reapeth
  All her heart, unknown remains.

Why, Kind JESU, why thus hiding,
  When Thyself Thou wouldst reveal?
Why, in Mary's breast abiding,
  From her love Thyself conceal?
Why, True Light, in her residing,
  Can she not Its radiance feel?

Oh, how strangely Thou eludest
  Souls that on Thee have believ'd!
But eluding, ne'er deludest,
  Nor deceiv'st, nor art deceiv'd;
But including, still excludest;
  Fully known, yet not perceiv'd.

Laud to Thee, and praise for ever,
  Life, Hope, Light of ev'ry soul!
Through Thy merits may we never
  Be inscrib'd in Death's dark roll,
But with Mary's true endeavour
  All our sins, like her, condole!   Amen.

Tandem fluctus, tandem luctus.

This elegant little Advent Hymn can scarcely be
earlier than the fifteenth century.

Storm and terror, grief and error,
  Comes the Sun to chase away:
And the morning fast adorning
  All the sky proclaims the day.

O true splendour, bright and tender,
  Sun of Righteousness on high,
Port Thou showest, source Thou owest
  To the Virgin's purity!

Now Thou keepest rest and sleepest
  In that zodiac of delight:
Joy hereafter shall with laughter
  Hail the coming Monarch's sight.

Satan, gnashing, sees it flashing
   Through that cloud so pure and white :
Thou endurest ever purest,
   Virgin Mother of the Light.

Darkness scattered, hell gates shattered,
   Victory to the souls draws nigh,
Whom confession of transgression
   Justly had condemned to die.

Earth rejoices : heavenly voices
   Render praise to GOD above ;
Now renewing and bedewing
   Every soul with fuller love.   Amen.

Attolle paullum lumina.

The following hymns are clearly of the very latest date : certainly not earlier than the sixteenth, it may be the beginning of the seventeenth, century. Their intensely subjective character would be a sufficient proof of this : and their rhyme equally shows it. Feminine double rhymes, in almost all mediæval hymns, are reserved for trochaic measures ;—their use, as here, in iambics, gives a certain impression of irreverence which it is hard to get over. Notwithstanding the wide difference between these and mediæval hymns, they possess, I think, considerable beauty : and perhaps will be more easily appreciated by modern readers.

RAISE, raise thine eyes a little way,
 O sinful man, discerning
Thy sins, how great and foul are they,
 And to repentance turning :
  On the Crucified One look,—
  Thou shalt read as in a book,
What well is worth thy learning.

Look on the Head, with such a Crown
  Of bitter thorns surrounded ;
Look on the Blood that trickles down
  The Feet and Hands thus wounded !
    Let that frame thy tears engage,
    Marking how Judæa's rage
  And malice hath abounded.

But though upon Him many a smart
  Its bitterness expendeth,
Yet more,—oh how much more !—His Heart
  Man's thankless spirit rendeth !
    On the Cross, bewailed by none,
    Mark, O man, how Mary's Son
  His life of sorrow endeth.

None ever bare such grief, alas,
  None ever such affliction,
As when Judæa brought to pass
  His bitter crucifixion :
    He, that we might dwell on high,
    Bare the pangs that made Him die
  In oft-renewed infliction.

O therefore Satan's wiles repel,
  And yield not to temptation !
Think on the woes that CHRIST befell
  In working thy salvation !

For, if He had never died,
  What could thee and all betide
But uttermost damnation?

If thus He bled, that Only Son
  The FATHER held so dearly,
Thou wicked servant, faithless one,
  O how much more severely!
    If the green wood kindled, how
    Shall not every sapless bough
Consume as fuel merely!

O mortal! heed these terrors well!
  O sinner, flee from sinning!
Consider thou the woes of hell,
  Ne'er ending, still beginning:
    Render thanks to CHRIST on high:
    Thus with Him beyond the sky
Eternal glory winning.   Amen.

[Inserted in *Hymns Ancient and Modern*, with the
alteration of the two trochaic into iambic lines; an
improvement on the original metre.]

Exite, Sion Filiae.[1]

DAUGHTERS of Sion, see your King!
 Go forth, go forth to meet Him!
Your Solomon is hastening
 Where that dear flock shall greet Him!
The sceptre and the crown by right
He wears, in robe of purple dight.

Your Solomon, the Prince of Peace,
 Bears not His Mother's laurel:
But with the olive bids to cease
 The long and bloody quarrel:
JESUS, the SON of GOD Most High,
Offers His peace to them that die.

It glitters fair, His Diadem,
 But Thorns are there entwining:

And from the Red sea comes each gem
  That in its wreath is shining :
Their radiance glows like stars at night :
With precious blood-drops are they bright.

The Royal Sceptre that He bears
  Beneath Whom nature quaketh,
No monarch's pride and pomp declares,
  A Reed, it feebly shaketh :
For iron sceptre ne'er possess'd
The power to guide a human breast.

The Festive Purple of the LORD,
  Is here no garment stately :
A vest, by very slaves abhorred ;
  —The worm hath tinged it lately :[3]
"I am a Worm," of old said He,—
And what its toils have tinged, ye see.

We therefore to the King of kings
  Bow lowly, from Him learning
The pomp and pride that this world brings
  To make our boast in spurning :
Such love the members best adorns,
For whom the Head was crowned with
    thorns.   Amen.

[1] There is another, but inferior hymn, with the same commencement. The reference, it need hardly be said, is to Canticles iii. 11.

[2] This very, perhaps too, bold metaphor is very seldom employed elsewhere in mediæval poetry. In the Compline Hymn for Whit-Sunday in the Sarum Breviary, among other titles of our LORD, we find

Agnus, Ovis, Vitulus, Serpens, Aries, Leo, *Vermis*.

Huc ad jugum Calvariae.

A poem of the same character, and probably of the
same date as the last. I know it only from Daniel's
Hymnology. Vol. II. p. 353.

UP to the Hill of Calvary
 With CHRIST our LORD ascending,
We deem that Cross our victory
 'Neath which His knees are bending :—
What soldier is of generous strain?
 One honour let him cherish ;—
With CHRIST upon the battle plain
 A thousand times to perish !

On must the faithful warrior go
 Whereso the Chief precedeth ;
And all true hearts will seek the foe
 Where'er the Banner leadeth ;—
Our highest victory,—it is loss :
 No cup hath such completeness
Of gall, but that remembered Cross
 Will turn it into sweetness !

Doth sickness hover o'er thy head,
  In weakness art thou lying?
Behold upon the Cross's bed
  Thy sick Physician dying!
No member in the holy frame
  That there for thee must languish,
But what thy pride hath clothed with shame,—
  But what thy sin, with anguish!

Have wealth and honour spread their wing
  And left thee all unfriended?—
See naked on the Cross thy King,—
  And thy regrets are ended:
The fox hath where to lay his head,
  Her nest receives the sparrow:
Thy Monarch, for His latest bed,
  One plank hath, hard and narrow!

Thy good name suffers from the tongue
  Of slanderers and oppressors?
JESUS, as on the Cross He hung,
  Was reckoned with transgressors!
More than the nails and than the spear
  His sacred limbs assailing,
Judæa's children pierced His ear
  With blasphemy and railing.

Fear'st thou the death that comes to all,
  And knows no interceder?—
O glorious struggle!—thou wilt fall,
  The soldier by the Leader!
CHRIST went with death to grapple first,
  And vanquished him before thee:
His darts then, let him do his worst,
  Can win no triumph o'er thee!

And, if thy conscience brands each sense
  With many a past defilement,
Here, by the fruits of penitence,
  Hope thou for reconcilement!
For He, Who bowed His holy Head,
  In death serenely sleeping,
Hath grace on contrite hearts to shed,
  And pardon for the weeping!   Amen.

Triumphe! plaudant maria.

SING victory, O ye seas and lands!
Ye floods and rivers, clap your hands!
Break forth in joy, angelic bands!
Crown ye the King That midst you stands,
To Whom the Heavenly gate expands!
  Bow before His Name Eternal
  Things celestial, things terrestrial,
  And infernal.

Sing victory, Angel guards that wait!
Lift up, lift up the Eternal gate,
And let the King come in with state!
And, as ye meet Him on the way,
The mighty triumph greet, and say,
Hail! JESU! glorious Prince, to-day!
  Bow before His Name Eternal
  Things celestial, things terrestrial,
  And infernal.

Who is the King of glory blest
Effulgent in His purple vest ?
With garments dyed in Bosrah, He
Ascends in pomp and jubilee.
It is the King, renowned in fight,
Whose hands have shattered Satan's might.
  Bow before His Name Eternal
  Things celestial, things terrestrial,
  And infernal.

Right gloriously strife endeth now !
Henceforward all things to Thee bow,
And, at the FATHER's Side sit Thou !
O JESU, all our wishes' goal,
Be Thou our joy when troubles roll,
And the reward of every soul !
  Bow before His Name Eternal
  Things celestial, things terrestrial,
  And infernal.

J. MASTERS AND CO., PRINTERS, ALDERSGATE STREET.

ADDITIONS AND CORRECTIONS.

Page 148, instead of the verse:

> Here his bride Urias loses, &c.

read as follows: (I am indebted for the alteration to the Dean of Westminster:)

> Here his wife Urias loses,
> Bathsheba, whom David chooses,
>   To a queen's estate to bring:
> Than the royal maidens fairer,
> She, of gold-wrought raiment wearer,
>   ' Shall be brought unto the King.'

Page 154, instead of:

> Ever Virgin, pregnant ever,
> Youth and age disjoining never, &c.

read:

> Ever Virgin, ever bearing,
> Youth and age for ever sharing, &c.

At page 123, add to the note about Leviathan: And so Adam of S. Victor:

> Sic hamum divinitatis
>   Occultat mortalitas:
> Sic voracis Leviathan
>   Luditur voracitas;

Qui dum capit glutiendum
Nostri vermem generis,
Ipse captus inescatur;
Pax est data posteris;

where, however, observe that the metaphor is not exactly the same. In the former passage the bait applies more immediately to our LORD's Human Nature, considered relatively to the Hypostatic Union: in the latter Adam would rather take the whole human race as the bait, the Hook of Divinity being the same in both.

WORKS ON HYMNOLOGY,

HYMNS FOR CHILDREN. In three Series. 3d. each, or bound together, 1s.

HYMNS FOR THE SICK. Second Edition. Price 6d.; cloth, 1s.

SONGS AND BALLADS FOR MANUFACTURERS. Price 3d.

LAYS AND LEGENDS OF THE CHURCH IN ENG-LAND. 2s. 6d.

COMMENTARY ON THE WORDS OF THE HYMNAL NOTED. Part I. 18mo., 6d.

THE RHYTHM OF BERNARD DE MORLAIX, Monk of Cluny, on the Celestial Country. Fourth edition. 8d.

HYMNS OF THE EASTERN CHURCH, with Notes and an Introduction. Second Edition. 2s. 6d.

SEQUENTIÆ EX MISSALIBUS GERMANICIS, ANGLICIS, GALLICIS, ALIISQUE MEDII ÆVI, COLLECTÆ. Recensuit, notulisque instruxit, JOANNES M. NEALE, S.T.P. 7s.

EPISTOLA CRITICA DE SEQUENTIIS: Tomo V. Thesauri Hymnologici a H. A. DANIEL editi prefixa. Lipsiæ, 1856.

HYMNI ECCLESIÆ: e Breviariis quibusdam et Missalibus Gallicanis, Germanis, Hispanicis, Lusitanis, desumpti. Oxonii, 1850.